Tying the Knot

Symbolic Ceremonies to Celebrate Your Union

TRADITIONS~RITUALS~CUSTOMS

What to do and what to say for the ceremony within your ceremony

Marty Younkin

Tying the Knot

Symbolic Ceremonies to Celebrate Your Union

Marty Younkin

1st Edition
©2017 by Marty Younkin
All rights reserved.
Printed and bound in USA.
First Printing, July 2017

Editor: Beth Schmidt B&J design

Cover Designer: Lauren Kerrigan

Illustrator: McKenna Reyna

Publisher: Love Notes

Thank you to those who gave permission to use their material, especially those who allowed alterations and adaptations. Credits and permissions are listed on the Acknowledgments page.

ISBN: 978-0-9668745-6-3 (print book)
ISBN: 978-0-9668745-5-6 (ebook)
LCCN: 2017905194
Published by LoveNotes, Sachse, TX

Love Notes

www.lovenotesweddings.com

Preface

Tying the knot before your family and friends can either be a magnificent or a mediocre experience for both you and your guests. When you include a symbolic ceremony, it gives your wedding that extra special touch that sets it apart from other wedding ceremonies. Your guests may not remember much from the rest of the service, but they will remember the tradition, ritual or custom you performed during the ceremony because it is a visual symbol of your union and a personal reflection of who you are as a couple.

I chose to write this book because, even though one can find information about traditions, rituals and customs elsewhere, it is sometimes difficult to find the words or the script to accompany them. The brides whose weddings I officiate always ask me to "write pretty words" to go with their symbolic ceremony. Some of the accompanying scripts in this book are my words, and some were given to me by the couples whose weddings I have performed. I have compiled 55 rituals—some old and some new, with a script, procedure instructions, and the items you will need for each one. Now you will know exactly what to say, what to do, and what you need for a symbolic ceremony within your ceremony.

As you read through the book, please note that words in bold should be substituted with proper names, e.g., **Groom**, **Bride**, **Children**, **Parents**, **Groom's Mother**, **Bride's Mother**, **Honoree**, **Designated Individual**.

There are many different traditions, rituals and customs from which to choose. Find one that fits you and captures the spirit of what is important to you as a couple so your family and friends can share in your love in a more meaningful way.

Colin Cowie, wedding expert, expressed his feelings about incorporating rituals into a wedding ceremony this way: "I love 'ritual' and have a deep respect of what it can do for us. Rituals add extra layers of meaning to milestones in our lives and give the people we love insight into who we are and what is important to us. They might include a family tradition passed down from generation to generation, a religious custom, or an experience from your travels you want to share with your friends and family. No matter what its inspiration, adding ritual to the ceremony turns a collection of many individuals into a single united congregation."

Marty Younkin

Table of Contents

A Mother's Kiss

First Kiss~Last Kiss

(Honoring Mothers of Bride and Groom)

A MOTHER'S KISS *(First Kiss~Last Kiss~Honoring Mothers)*

"A Mother's Kiss" is a very tender and emotional moment between mother and child toward the end of the wedding ceremony before "the kiss" between the Bride and Groom. It also may be done during the Unity Candle or other unity ceremony where mothers participate. Roses also may be given to the mothers after they kiss and hug their children.

(Officiant): We wish to honor the mothers of the Bride and Groom during this next part of the ceremony. **Bride's Mother** and **Groom's Mother**, will you come and stand by your child?

(Both mothers come forward and stand next to their child.)

(Officiant to mothers): The Bride and Groom wish to honor you and thank you for the unconditional love you have given to them their whole life long. You are the "unsung hero," and they recognize the sacrifices you have made in order to nurture and enrich their lives, making them into the individuals they are today. However, I know you would say that being a mother is not about what you gave up to have a child, but what you have gained by having one.

(Officiant to mothers): The Bible says, "Children are a gift from the Lord; they are a reward from Him" *(Ps. 127:3 NLT)*, and you accept that gift with all your heart. You have given these children both roots and wings—roots to remind them where they came from, and wings to show them what they can become. It is because of you that they stand here today, ready to follow in your footsteps and take the next step of their journey—marriage. We, as guests, are witness to this joyous occasion, and we owe it all to a mother's love.

(Song, "A Mother's Love" by Jim Brickman may be inserted here—very effective. May be played on cd or shown on screen as found on YouTube. Warning: It's a tearjerker!)

(Officiant): Never underestimate the power of "a mother's love." One of the most beautiful quotes I have ever heard about a mother's love was found in a note written by a mother to her child. It said this: "No one else will ever know the strength of my love for you. After all, you're the only one who knows what my heart sounds like from the inside. Love, Mom."

At this time, we will share in a very special moment with the Bride and Groom and their mothers. These mothers' lips were the first to kiss them as babies when they brought them into this world and gave them life. And these mothers' lips will be the last to kiss them as singles before they are united in marriage and seal that union with their own first kiss. Today, a mother's love, together with her blessings, will be first to send them on their way to their new life together as husband and wife. **Bride's** mother and **Groom's** mother will now share a kiss with their children. Mothers, one last time before your "babies" are married—you may kiss the Bride and Groom!

(Hugs and kisses are exchanged between Bride and her mother and Groom and his mother. Roses or symbolic jewelry also may be given to mothers here. Mothers are then seated.)

Quotes about Mothers *(optional)*

No one else will ever know the strength of my love for you. After all, you are the only one who knows what my heart sounds like from the inside.~*Unknown*

Mother love is the fuel that enables a normal human being to do the impossible.~*C. Garretty*

There is an instinct in a woman to love most her own child—and an instinct to make any child who needs her love, her own.~*Robert Brault*

A Mother is she who can take the place of all others, but whose place no one else can take.
~*Unknown*

A Mother holds her children's hands for a short while, but their hearts forever.~*Unknown*

Did you ever notice that MOM spelled upside down is WOW?!~*Unknown*

Her children rise up and call her blessed.~*Proverbs 31:28 NKJV*

Note: Youtube link to **"A Mother's Love"** song by Jim Brickman
http://tinyurl.com/hmc4ccc

You will need:
"A Mother's Love" CD by Jim Brickman *(optional)*

Bible~Coins~Lasso~Veil

La Biblia~Las Arras~El Lazo~El Velo

(Hispanic/Filipino)

BIBLE~COINS~LASSO~VEIL
(la Biblia~las Arras~el Lazo~el Velo~Hispanic/Filipino)

The "Bible, Coins, Lasso and Veil" (la Biblia, las Arras, el Lazo y el Velo) are traditions most often associated with the Catholic Church and Hispanic weddings. However, Filipinos use variations of these traditions also. They are symbolic of the spiritual, physical and emotional elements in a marriage. The Bible (la Biblia) symbolizes religious guidance and wise counsel for life's decisions, while the Veil (el Velo) illustrates God's love and protection over their marriage —both spiritual elements. The thirteen Coins (las Arras), like a dowry, represent the financial support and blessings for their home—physical element. The Lasso (el Lazo) signifies the union of their hearts, souls and lives into one common destiny—emotional element.

Hispanic Traditions

Bible *(la Biblia)~Spiritual element*
(After Bride and Groom exchange vows and rings, Sponsors or Padrinos bring the Holy Bible and rosary beads and place them in hands of Bride and Groom.)

(As couple holds Bible, Officiant blesses it): Lord, bless this Bible and the lives of those who read it. We know the Holy Bible is the Word of God. We pray that it may be the spiritual guide that will light **Groom** and **Bride's** pathway and will guide them in all their decisions so that their will and God's will are one. Amen. *(Sponsors take Holy Bible and rosary beads and sit down.)*

Coins *(las Arras)~Physical element*
(Coin Sponsors bring forth box of coins and empty it into Groom's hands.)

(Officiant explains symbolism of coins): These thirteen coins are a symbol of the care that **Groom** and **Bride** will give in order for their home to have everything it needs. These coins also are a sign of the blessings of God and all the good things they will share together.

(Officiant blesses coins): Lord, may these coins be a symbol of your provision and favor throughout **Groom's** and **Bride's** lives. Provide them with all they need for their home and family. We give you thanks for all the good things they are going to share because of your many blessings, Lord. Amen.

(Groom drops coins into Bride's hands.)

(Groom): **Bride**, receive these thirteen coins as a symbol of my dedication in caring for our home and providing for our family's necessities.

(Bride): **Groom**, I accept your gift of dedication, and I promise on my part that everything provided will be used with care for the benefit of our home and family. *(Sponsors take coins, place them back in box and sit down.)*

Lasso *(el Lazo)~Emotional element*

(Lasso Sponsors bring forth lasso and place it around shoulders of kneeling or standing Bride and Groom in a figure eight, which symbolizes eternity.)

(Officiant): **Groom** and **Bride**, this lasso has been placed around you in a figure eight, which symbolizes eternity. It represents the ties that bind you together—the union of two hearts into one heart, two souls into one soul, and two lives into one life.

(Officiant blesses union): O Lord, bless this couple as they journey through life together. Unite them into one spirit…hand in hand, heart to heart, flesh to flesh, and soul to soul. Amen.

(Sponsors remove lasso and sit down unless veil ceremony is included here; if so, lasso remains until veil ceremony is concluded.)

Veil *(el Velo)~Spiritual element*

(Sponsors bring forth veil and place it over Brides's head and Groom's shoulders and pin to clothes. Note that in a Filipino wedding, veil ceremony goes before lasso ceremony.)

(Officiant): This veil, or mantel, covers the Bride and Groom today, reminding them that Christ covers us with his love. Their new home will be a place where God dwells because they choose to live under the mantel of his love and protection.

(Officiant prays): Lord, as **Groom** and **Bride** join their lives in marriage, cover them with your love as this veil covers them now. Protect them, strengthen them and guide them throughout all their days together. And may they always choose to live under the mantel of your love. Amen.

(Sponsors remove veil [and lasso] and sit down.)

You will need for both the Hispanic and Filipino traditions:
- Bible
- thirteen gold or silver coins in a decorative box or bag
- lasso, cord (or double rosary)
- veil (pins or clips to hold veil in place)
- rosary beads *(optional)*

Filipino Traditions

Coins *(Arras or Arrhae)~Blessings of God/Financial support*

The blessing of the coins symbolizes both God's blessings and the husband's dedication and responsibility to his wife and children. The Groom presents the coins to his Bride who accepts them, showing her support and commitment to their union.

(Sponsors bring coins forward and place in Bride's and Groom's hands.)

(Officiant): **Groom** and **Bride**, these coins are a symbol of God's provision and blessings for your home and family. Hold these coins in your hands as a sign that your blessings no longer will be held separately, but together. Remember, the gifts you receive in this life are not truly yours, but God's. As guardians of God's gifts, use them well.

(Officiant prays): Lord, may these coins be a symbol of your provision and favor throughout **Groom's** and **Bride's** lives. Provide them with all they need for their home and family. We give you thanks for all the good things they are going to share because of your many blessings. Amen.

Veil *(Belo)~God's protection over marriage*
(Veil covers Bride's head, its edge is placed over Groom's shoulders, covering his back, then pinned.)

(Officiant): The veil is placed over the Bride and Groom to demonstrate their union for life under one roof. The laying of the veil symbolizes the purity and honesty of marriage, and invokes God's protection over their union made here today.

(Officiant prays): Dear Lord, with the purest of threads, you have spun a fine veil of love over **Groom** and **Bride**. Keep this precious mantle whole and immaculate; mend the tears of trials and hardship with fibers of strength; and wash away the stains of anger and distrust with the waters of forgiveness and faith. Amen.

Cord *(Lasso)~Ties that bind couple together*
(One strand of cord is placed over Bride's shoulders and the other over Groom's shoulders, with knot between them. Cord resembles double rosary.)

(Officiant): This cord symbolizes the ties that bind your hearts and souls together through the love of God. It represents the union of your two hearts into one heart, two souls into one soul, and two lives into one life. May your love grow stronger and bind you closer together through the years, from this day until eternity.

(Officiant prays): Dear Lord, as the cord of unity is wrapped around **Groom and Bride**, we ask you to continue to bind them together in love. You have entwined their lives and fortified their bond with your Spirit. With you, Lord, they are a three-fold cord that cannot be broken—one strength, one life, one love. Amen.

Blended Family Gift Presentation

Family Medallion~Other Symbolic Gift

(Participation of children in ceremony)

BLENDED FAMILY GIFT PRESENTATION
(Family Medallion~Other symbolic gift~Participation of children in ceremony)

More than one in four marriages involve children. Many couples come together with children of their own or from previous relationships. Studies show that children accept a parent's marriage more readily when they are included in the wedding plans and given a tangible symbol of being embraced by the new family. Most children do not usually care what the symbol is, as long as it is personal, perhaps engraved, and acknowledges their significance in the new family being created.

A very popular gift is jewelry. There are many styles of blended family symbolic jewelry—a pendant or necklace, a bracelet, a charm, a ring, earrings, a pin or tie tack, a key chain, a watch or a dog tag. Most of these may be engraved with names and dates, if you wish.

During this part of the ceremony, the children will come forward and form a circle or semi-circle with the Bride and Groom who welcome the children into the family and may verbally make a commitment to them with family vows. *(See Family Vows, page 61.)*

Presentation of Gifts to Children

(Children come and form circle or semi-circle with Bride and Groom. Children should face guests.)

(Officiant to children): Just as **Groom** and **Bride** gave each other rings as symbols of their love and commitment to one another, they also would like to present (each of) you with a gift as a symbol of their love and commitment to you.

(Officiant may describe and explain gift of symbolic jewelry and its meaning.)

(Bride and Groom present children with symbolic jewelry, and give each child a hug and a kiss. They also may say family vows to children at this time.)

(Officiant to children): **Child/ren,** whenever you look at your pendant (or other symbolic jewelry gift), it will always be a reminder that you belong to this family. But most importantly, it will remind you how very, very much you are loved.

(Children may be seated.)

Note: Blended family and other symbolic jewelry may be found in a variety of locations— **www.etsy.com, www.pinterest.com,** retail stores like **www.thingsremembered.com** or jewelry stores like **www.jamesavery.com.**

You will need:
- blended family jewelry or other symbolic jewelry or gift
- prepared family vows printed on cards

Family Medallion® Ceremony

This ceremony and its coordinating symbolic jewelry, created by Rev. Roger Coleman of Clergy Services, Inc., was designed to significantly include the children of those being married in the wedding celebration. The "Family Medallion®" provides a symbol for recognizing family relationships by adding a third circle, representing children, to the two Bride and Groom circles.

During this part of the ceremony, the children will come forward and form a circle or semi-circle with the Bride and Groom who welcome the children into the family and may verbally make a commitment to them with family vows. *(See Family Vows, page 61.)*

Presentation of Gifts to Children

(Children come and form circle or semi-circle with Bride and Groom. Children should face guests.)

(Officiant to children): Just as **Groom** and **Bride** gave each other rings as symbols of their love and commitment to one another, they also would like to present (each of) you with a gift as a symbol of their love and commitment to you.

For New Blended Families

(Officiant to guests): The Family Medallion® is made up of three intertwining circles, two of which symbolize the union of this man and woman in marriage. The third circle represents the joining of children to this union, making it complete as we celebrate the new family created today.

For Established Blended Families

(Officiant to guests): The Family Medallion® is made up of three intertwining circles, two of which symbolize the union of this man and woman in marriage. The third circle represents the joining of children to this union, making it complete as we celebrate the love of this family today.

(Bride and Groom present children with Family Medallion®, and give each child a hug and a kiss. They also may say family vows to children at this time.)

(Officiant to children): **Child/ren,** whenever you look at your Family Medallion®, it will always be a reminder that you belong to this family. But most importantly, it will remind you how very, very much you are loved.

(Children may be seated.)

Note: The Family Medallion® may be found at **www.familymedallion.com**.

You will need:
• Family Medallion jewelry

Blessing Of The Hands

BLESSING OF THE HANDS

(Officiant): **Groom** and **Bride**, your hands will play a very important role in your relationship as husband and wife. They are the physical extensions of your heart. As I share this blessing, please join your hands, and with your hands, your hearts.

(Bride and Groom clasp hands in figure eight "eternity knot" while Officiant shares blessing.)

These Hands

These are the hands of your best friend, young and strong and full of love, that hold yours
    on your wedding day as you promise to love each other all the days of your life.
These are the hands that will work along side yours as you build your future together.
These are the hands that will passionately love you and care for you throughout the years.
These are the hands that will hold you when fear or grief fills your mind,
    and, with the slightest touch, will comfort you like no other.
These are the hands that will give you strength when you struggle,
    and support and encouragement to chase down your dreams.
These are the hands that will tenderly hold your children,
    and help keep your family together as one.
These are the hands that will, countless times, wipe the tears from your eyes,
    tears of sorrow and tears of joy.
And lastly, these are the hands that, even when wrinkled with age, will still be reaching for yours,
    still giving you the same unspoken tenderness with just a touch—
        a touch from **These Hands.** *~Daniel L. Harris, revised*

Religious Blessing of the Hands

(Officiant): O God, bless these hands that are before you this day. May they always be held by one another. Give these hands the strength to hold on during the storms of stress and the dark of disillusionment. Keep them tender and gentle as they nurture each other in their wondrous love. Help these hands to continue building a relationship founded in your grace, rich in caring for your people, and devoted in reaching for your perfection. May you always hold **Groom** and **Bride** in the palm of your hand, loving them, protecting them, and guiding them in the way they should go. Amen.

Non-religious Blessing of the Hands

(Officiant): May these hands always be held by one another. Give them the strength to hold on during the storms of stress and the dark of disillusionment. Keep them tender and gentle as they nurture each other in their wondrous love. Help these hands to continue building a relationship founded on mutual respect, rich in caring for each other's needs, and devoted to fulfilling each other's dreams. May their hands always continue to reach out for one another, and when no words can be found, may a touch from these hands say "I love you and I am here—now, forever and always."

Blessing Stones

Wishing Stones

BLESSING STONES *(Wishing Stones)*

Blessing Stones~Version 1
(Blessing Stones combined in container)

(Each guest is given a small stone upon arriving. Markers may be provided to write blessing words on stones.)

(Officiant): **Groom** and **Bride**, before you met, your lives were on different paths with different destinations. But love brought you together and joined your separate paths into one. Today, your families and friends will be joined also, symbolized now with the "Blessing Stones" ceremony.

Each of your guests have been given a stone that represents their relationship with you and their presence at your wedding today. Both of you also have a stone of your own that symbolizes your previous separate lives, separate sets of friends, separate families and the different life's journeys you once traveled.

I will ask each of you to take the stone you hold, and make a wish or say a blessing for **Groom** and **Bride,** and for the new life they begin together as husband and wife.

(Everyone pauses to make their wish or say a blessing.)

(Officiant): Now we will collect the stones from your family and friends and place them in a special container. *(These stones have words written on them so you may see all your blessings.)*

(Stones are collected and placed in container.)

(Officiant): The Bride and Groom will now add their individual stones to the container as well.

(Couple adds their stones to container.)

(Officiant): With the combining of these stones, you have symbolically joined your once separate lives. As all the stones have been combined with love into one container, so also are your families and friends joined, through you, into one. Your once solitary life's paths are now one path also. All that once was separate is now shared, and in this sharing you both will find new strength and joy as you forge a new life's path together.

Blessing Stones~Version 2
(Blessing Stones with note cards)

The ritual of the "Blessing Stones," or "Wishing Stones," as they sometimes are called, is a wonderful way to include everyone in the wedding by way of offering blessings and good wishes to the newlyweds. It also is a good way to ensure everyone will make contact with the Bride and Groom at some point during the day. This ritual may be performed at the actual ceremony itself (before the blessing), or at the conclusion of the service (in a receiving line manner), or later at the reception.

When the guests arrive at the ceremony, they are given a Blessing Stone along with a note card with words printed on it such as: "My wish for you is…" or "May you be blessed with…" or "May God bless you with…"

(During ceremony, Officiant explains significance of Blessing Stones.)

(Officiant): Today is a very blessed occasion in the lives of **Groom** and **Bride**. You have been invited here today because of your special relationship with them. When you arrived, you received a stone along with a note card. These are called "Blessing Stones." Since we all desire nothing but the best life has to offer this couple, I ask you to complete the sentence on the card and sign your name so your best wishes and blessings for **Groom** and **Bride** may always be a reminder of your love for them on this day of celebration.

(At some point, either during or after service, guests will share blessing or wish with newlyweds and toss Blessing Stone into Blessing Bowl, Wishing Well, Fountain or whatever is chosen to hold water. They may place "love note" into basket or box for couple to reflect on at a later time.)

Many couples keep their Blessing Stones in a special place in their home (a vase of flowers, around a candle, in an aquarium or terrarium) to remind them of all the love, good wishes and blessings they share because of their family and friends.

Blessing Stones ~ Version 3

(Blessing Stones thrown in body of water)

(Stones either are gathered at site or provided for guests. After ceremony, everyone follows Bride and Groom's recessional to water, makes a wish or offers a blessing for them and casts their stone into water as Officiant closes ceremony with following words.)

(Officiant): Please make a wish or offer a blessing for the Bride and Groom. Then you may toss your Blessing Stone into the water. *(Guests toss stones in water.)*

(Officiant): The ripples made in the water represent the love and good wishes not only for this couple, but for all the world. For as our ripples cross and recross one another's, so our love and good wishes touch and retouch all those around us and all those with whom we come into contact throughout our lives.

You will need:
- Stones~you may use decorative stones, rose quartz stones (which symbolize love), gems or crystals, pebbles from a special place or river rocks that can be written upon with a marker
- Container~you will need a Blessing Bowl (any decorative basin, bowl, bucket will work), or a table top fountain or wishing well to hold the water
- Basket~you will need a decorative note card holder
- Love Notes~buy or make decorative note cards and print your opening blessing phrase on them. Begin your phrase with: "My wish for you is…" or "May you be blessed with…" or "May God bless you with…" Provide pens to write notes; markers to write on stones

Blessing Tree

Wishing Tree

BLESSING TREE *(Wishing Tree)*

Love Notes~Good Wishes~Blessings on Branches of Tree

For couples wanting to bring a little bit of nature into their ceremony, the "Blessing Tree" or "Wishing Tree" is a unique option.

If a real tree is to be used, it should be a sapling of no more than shoulder height. Most couples, however, use an imitation tree or collection of branches or branch-like structures.

In mid-ceremony, after the exchange of vows and rings, the Officiant invites the VIPs (parents, family members, close friends) to come up and affix a blessing or wish to the tree. Actually, it need not be a blessing or wish *per se*; it could be poetry, a personal note, a religious passage, a quotation or song lyrics. They may choose to read the blessing out loud at that time or simply place it on the tree for the couple to read later.

(Officiant): **Groom** and **Bride** have chosen to include a "Blessing Tree" ritual in their ceremony. Since we all love this couple and want the best for them, let's add our best wishes and blessings to their Blessing Tree so they always will be reminded of the love of their family and friends. At this time, I would like to invite some very important people, who are special to the Bride and Groom, to come forward and place their blessings on the Blessing Tree. During the reception, all of you will be given the opportunity to share a blessing, a wish, a poem, a scripture, or some advice on a notecard. Then you will attach your love note to the Blessing Tree.

(VIPs place notes on tree.)

(Officiant): May the Blessing Tree be a reminder of the love and good wishes you have been blessed with from your family and friends on your wedding day and always.

(Having affixed their blessings to the tree, the VIPs embrace the Bride and Groom. Alternatively, the couple is the first to affix a blessing to the tree, which typically is their personally composed vows—a lovely touch. The couple then may give roses to the VIPs, if desired.)

During the reception, every guest has, at their place setting, a card with an attached loop string. Throughout the evening, the guests will compose their notes to the couple and attach their notes to the tree. By the evening's end, there will be several love notes on the branches of the tree, which will go into the wedding photo album along with the photos of those who wrote them.

(If a live tree is used, it is planted after honeymoon. If so, Officiant will close with these words.)

(Officiant): The Bride and Groom will plant this Blessing Tree in their yard. As it matures, it will shade them and their new home, its changing colors marking the seasons as well, and its beauty reminding them of the love and well wishes once borne on its branches.

You will need:
- imitation tree (or live sapling)
- note cards with ribbons or cords for attaching to tree
- pens or markers for guests to write on cards

Wishing Tree Readings (optional)

Gift of Advice

From each of your experiences
    comes a very treasured gift
A piece of hidden knowledge
    we didn't know exists
Please share with us your wisdom
    about marriage, love and life
How to be a loving husband
    or to be the perfect wife
Please write your thoughts and wishes
    it would be so very nice
For the greatest gift of all
    is the gift of your advice
        ~Unknown

The Wedding Wish Tree

Here stands our Wedding Wish Tree
Though it looks a little bare
But it would look so pretty
With the thoughts you want to share

So please pick up the pen and write
A thought, a joke, a quote
Then tie it to the branches
and watch your wishes float

And when this day is over
We can't wait to have a look
We will keep the little labels
In our Wedding Wish Tree Book

And in the years that follow
We'll remember on this day
All your thoughts and words so kind
And in our hearts you'll stay
        ~Unknown

Wishing Tree

As we begin our journey
    as a brand new Mr. and Mrs.
We could surely use
    your advice and good wishes

Share with us your wisdom
    about marriage, love and life
The secret to being a good husband
    or a top notch first rate wife

Jot down a memory
    or reminder of our day
A doodle or picture will do
    if you don't know what to say

Please don't forget
    it would be a shame
Don't hang your wish on our tree
    without signing your name

Whatever you pen
    we're sure to treasure
Long after this day has passed
    your words will bring us pleasure
        ~Unknown

Branding Ceremony

(Western/Cowboy)

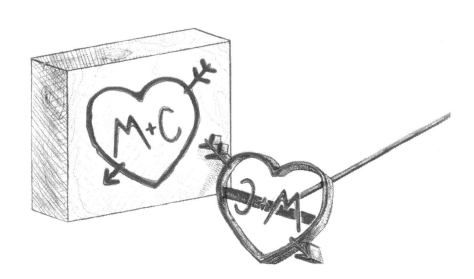

BRANDING CEREMONY *(Western/Cowboy)*

(Officiant): Today, **Groom** and **Bride** are celebrating their union with a "Branding Ceremony." As a sign of their love, the intertwining of their lives, and the fire that burns within their souls for each other, they will brand this piece of wood (or, piece of cowhide mounted on wood or any other medium chosen for the branding) with their uniquely designed brand.

You have heard the phrase "Ride for the brand?" Well, wranglers that work on a ranch will protect that ranch's brand through all adversity, and they will "ride for the brand" just as a couple will "ride" for their new brand, "marriage," protecting it from anything and everything that might work against it.

This brand will be on permanent display in their home to show their devotion to each other today, tomorrow and forever. If they ever get lost out on the range of life, it will be there to help them find their way back home again. It also will serve to remind them of the love and support you have given them on this special day and will continue to give them throughout their lives together.

At this time, I want to honor the parents and grandparents of the Bride and Groom, and to thank them for the values and ethics they branded on the lives of these two individuals, making them who they are today. And now, as you two move on together to blaze a trail of new traditions, never forget who you are and where you came from, for it is those things that drew you to each other and made you fall in love with one another in the first place.

(Bride and Groom brand wood, leather or whatever medium they have chosen.)

(Officiant): As this brand can never be undone, neither can your promise to each other ever be unspoken. May this brand always be a symbol of the love you share that has been burned in your souls and branded on your hearts forever and ever.

Branding Ceremony Procedure

(Brand waits in fire for the proper time. Couple place their hands on brand handle and press down on it to make impression on wood (or other medium chosen). Fire and smoke are key elements to capturing moment on film.)

Note: The brand you design can be anything you wish—your new married name, monogram or a configuration of your two last names, your wedding date, a scripture reference or a symbol meaningful to you. The brand also can be burned onto anything you desire such as a bench, a board, a plaque, a piece of cowhide or metal. This ceremony may be performed during the wedding service or at the reception.

You will need:
- branding iron in fire
- wood, leather or other medium to brand
- goggles *(optional)*

Breaking Bread

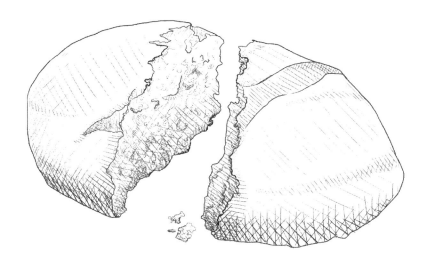

BREAKING BREAD

Many cultures use the "Breaking Bread" tradition in weddings to symbolize the joining of families and fellowship with one another. Poland, Bulgaria, Russia, Romania, Germany, and many slavic countries are among those cultures.

Christians have a "Breaking Bread" sacrament called "Communion" or "The Lord's Supper," which commemorates Christ's atonement on the cross for the sins of man. This is a very meaningful part of a Christian wedding ceremony, and many Brides and Grooms want to share Communion as their first act together as husband and wife. *(See Holy Communion, page 79.)*

Poland~Bread and Salt and Wine Blessing

(Officiant): The "Bread and Salt and Wine Blessing" is an old Polish tradition, which symbolizes the union of the Bride and Groom and their families. It is a blessing given to the couple by their parents for a long, happy and healthy life together.

(Parents bring forth loaf of bread, bowl of salt and goblet of wine. Parents sprinkle bread with salt and offer bread to couple to eat.)

(Officiant): **Groom** and **Bride**, your parents wish to offer a special blessing today because they want nothing but the very best for you as you share your life together. Now, as you partake of this bread they have blessed you with, it symbolizes their hope that you never will experience hunger and that all your needs will be met abundantly. The salt that was sprinkled on the bread represents the difficult times and challenges in life, which you, no doubt, will encounter, but must learn to cope with and confront together.

(Officiant blesses couple): May you be blessed with the bread of abundance and seasoned with the salt of life.

(Bride and Groom each tear off piece of bread and eat.)

(Parents then offer goblet of wine to couple.)

(Officiant): **Groom** and **Bride**, your parents bless you with the gift of wine with the hope that you never will thirst. It is their prayer that you will be blessed with good health and good cheer, and always share the company of many good friends.

(Bride and Groom each sip from goblet of wine.)

(Parents give hugs and kisses to Bride and Groom as a sign of love and unity, and welcome them into the family.)

(Officiant): May you break bread together and share fellowship with each other on many happy occasions throughout your lives.

Bulgaria~Pitka Bread and Honey Tradition

(Officiant): The Bride and Groom will share in the "Pitka Bread and Honey" tradition, an old Bulgarian custom. The sharing of the Pitka bread represents the welcoming of the Bride and Groom into each other's families. Mothers, will you please come and offer the bread and honey to **Groom** and **Bride**?

(Mother of Groom offers bread with honey to Bride, welcoming her into their family and wishing her a happy wedded life. Bride dips bread in honey and eats. Mother of Bride does same for Groom and Groom dips bread in honey and eats.)

(Officiant): **Groom** and **Bride**, will you each offer the bread and honey to your mothers-in-law to show your love and respect for your new families?

(Bride offers bread to her mother-in-law, while Groom does same for his mother-in-law.)

(Officiant): This next part of the ceremony, the breaking of the Pitka bread in two, will determine who the head of the household is. Whoever breaks off the largest half is the winner and claims the title of "breadwinner."

(Couple places loaf of bread over heads, holding it with a firm grip. On count of three, they pull on bread and tear it in two pieces. Guests cheer when "breadwinner" is determined by size of bread piece.)

(Officiant): Well, we can see who the head of the household is now!

(Bride and Groom tear off two small pieces of bread of equal size and dip in honey to feed each other.)

(Officiant): Regardless of who the "breadwinner" is, they have chosen to share the bread equally with each other. And by dipping the bread in the honey, it symbolizes all the sweet things in life they will share together.

Breaking Bread~Universal Tradition

The following "Breaking Bread" traditions are more universal versions signifying hospitality, home and family, and the fellowship shared with one another. These versions may be used either for the couple only, or for the Bride and Groom who are blending families and wish to include family members. Any type of bread may be chosen and baked by either a bakery or a significant person in your life, which adds even more meaning to the ceremony.

Breaking Bread Universal Tradition~*Version 1*
(Couple only)

(Officiant): Today, **Groom** and **Bride** have chosen to symbolize the joining of their lives by breaking bread together and sharing it with one another. This bread was specially baked with love by **Name**, which makes this ceremony even more meaningful...and probably tastier, too.

Bread has come to symbolize the staples in life, the basic necessities, the fundamental nourishment our lives need to exist. But the Bible says, "Man shall not live by bread alone" *(Matthew 4:4 NKJV)*. That means we need more than just physical food to feed our bodies; we need spiritual food also. When you "break bread" together, it not only represents all the times you actually will sit at a table and share a physical meal, but also symbolizes the spiritual aspect of those times—the sweet fellowship, the blessed communion, the wholehearted sharing of yourselves with one another. These are the elements needed to "feed" your soul. They are just as important, or even more so, as the physical nourishment.

So, **Groom** and **Bride**, you may share in this first act of marriage by breaking bread together.

(Bride and Groom each take a piece of bread and eat it or feed each other.)

(Groom and Bride say to each other): As I share this bread with you, I also share my life with you.

(Officiant): The Bible says, "They broke bread in their homes and ate together with glad and humble hearts" *(Acts 2:46 NIV)*. Let me encourage you to do this often. There is nothing more precious than sitting around a table sharing food, fun and fellowship with one another and creating memories to last a lifetime, just as you have done here today.

Marriage will allow you a new environment to share your lives together, to break bread as husband and wife, standing together to face life and the world, hand in hand. Marriage is going to expand you as individuals, define you as a couple, and deepen your love for one another. As you grow in love together, may your marriage always include the breaking of bread with all those you love.

Breaking Bread Universal Tradition~*Version 2*
(Couple with family)

(When family is included, all those involved in the Breaking Bread Ceremony come and form a circle with Bride and Groom. Starting with Groom, he tears off a piece of bread, then gives bread to Bride, who tears off a piece. She gives bread to person next to her, who tears off a piece and hands bread to next person and so on, until all have a piece of bread in their hands.)

(Officiant): Today, **Groom** and **Bride** have chosen to symbolize the joining of their lives and that of their families by "Breaking Bread" together and sharing it with those they love. This bread was specially baked with love by **Name**, which makes this ceremony even more meaningful...and probably tastier, too.

Bread has come to symbolize the staples in life, the basic necessities, the fundamental nourishment our lives need to exist. But the Bible says, "Man shall not live by bread alone" *(Matthew 4:4 NKJV)*. That means we need more than just physical food to feed our bodies; we need spiritual food also. When you "break bread" together, it not only represents all the times you actually will sit at a table and share a physical meal, but also symbolizes the spiritual aspect of those times—the sweet fellowship, the blessed communion, the wholehearted sharing of yourselves with one another. These are the elements needed to "feed" your soul. They are just as important, or even more so, as the physical nourishment.

So, let's all make a commitment to "feed" each other and share our lives by breaking bread with one another.

(Everyone holds their piece of bread up and says vows to each other all together. Vows may be repeated after Officiant or everyone may be told beforehand what to say.)

(All): As I share this bread with you, I also share my life with you. *(All eat bread.)*

(Officiant): The Bible says, "They broke bread in their homes and ate together with glad and humble hearts" *(Acts 2:46 NIV)*. Let me encourage you to do this often. There is nothing more precious than sitting around a table sharing food, fun and fellowship with one another and creating memories to last a lifetime, just as you have done here today.

As you grow in your love together, may you always include "breaking bread" with all those you love and cherish.

You will need: *(depending on version used)*
• loaf of bread
• salt
• wine
• honey
• small plates
• napkins

Breaking Of The Glass

(Jewish)

BREAKING OF THE GLASS *(Jewish)*

The "Breaking of the Glass" is a Jewish tradition with much symbolism and many meanings. Following are a few of those meanings.

The Breaking of the Glass is:
- a symbol of the destruction of the Holy Temple in Jerusalem
- a reminder of the tragic losses the Jewish people have suffered
- a reminder that, even amidst joy, a broken world still needs our attention, and people less fortunate still require our care
- a reminder not only of sorrow, but also an expression of hope for a future free from all violence and hatred
- a representation of the fragility of human relationships, including marriage
- a warning that love, like glass, is fragile and must be protected
- a reminder that marriage changes the lives of individuals forever, and the vows, like the broken glass, are irrevocable

(After couple is pronounced husband and wife, glass or light bulb, wrapped in a cloth and placed in a silk bag, is laid by Groom's foot.)

(Officiant): We conclude this ceremony with the "Breaking of the Glass." In Jewish tradition, the Breaking of the Glass at a wedding is a symbolic prayer, and hope that your love for one another will remain until the pieces of the glass come together again, or in other words, that your love will last forever.

The fragile nature of the glass also represents the frailty of human relationships. It reminds us that we must treat each other with special care, for even the strongest of relationships is subject to disintegration. So love, like glass, is fragile and must be protected. The glass then, is broken to "protect" the marriage with this prayer: "May your bond of love be as difficult to break as it would be to put the pieces of this glass together again."

And finally, the Breaking of the Glass is a reminder that marriage changes the lives of individuals forever, and your wedding vows, like the broken glass, are irrevocable and permanent.

(Groom breaks glass with his foot and everyone shouts, "Mazel Tov!", which means "Good luck!" or "Congratulations!")

Although the glass is shattered, the covering contains the pieces. This represents the difficulties the Bride and Groom may face together, but which will remain contained by the unity they have created this day.

Note: This tradition usually takes place sometime after the pronouncement, either right before or right after the kiss.

You will need:
- goblet or light bulb (easier to break) wrapped in a cloth or placed in a bag

Butterfly Release

(Native American)

BUTTERFLY RELEASE *(Native American)*

(Officiant): Today we celebrate the love between **Groom** and **Bride** with a "Butterfly Release." The release of butterflies at a wedding ceremony symbolizes a new beginning and a long life together. The Chinese word for butterfly means "70 years," and therefore, the butterfly has become a symbol for a long life. So, as we release these butterflies, let us all make a wish for the Bride and Groom to have a long and happy life together.

(Officiant shares legend.)

American Indian Legend

According to an American Indian Legend—
If anyone desires a wish to come true,
    they must first capture a butterfly and whisper that wish to it.
Since a butterfly can make no sound,
    the butterfly can not reveal the wish to anyone but the Great Spirit who hears and sees all.
In gratitude for giving the beautiful butterfly its freedom,
    the Great Spirit will always grant the wish.
So, according to legend, by making a wish and giving the butterfly its freedom,
    the wish will be taken to the heavens and then be granted.

(Officiant): We have gathered together to grant this couple all our best wishes and are about to set these butterflies free in trust that all these wishes will be granted. Please whisper your wish to the butterfly now. On the count of three, release your butterfly. One, two, three…

(Butterflies are then released.)

(Officiant may share blessing or poem.)

Butterfly Readings (optional)

Butterfly Blessing

May the wings of the butterfly kiss the sun
And find your shoulder to light on,
To bring you luck, happiness and riches
Today, tomorrow and beyond.
                    ~Irish Blessing

Learn to Fly

Like a butterfly emerges
    And unfolds its graceful wings
A marriage grows and it develops
    With the love each partner brings
Your flight through life together
    Is what you make it, so reach high
Spread your wings and learn to soar
    As if with wings of a butterfly
Share together life's great adventure
    Now the two of you are one
Shower your lover with butterfly kisses
    Your infinite journey has just begun
Be a lover, friend and playmate
    Learn to listen, laugh and cry
God has given you your wings
    But, you teach each other how to fly *~Larry James*

Butterfly Quotes (optional)

Love is like a butterfly. It goes wherever it pleases and pleases wherever it goes. *~Unknown*

Beautiful and graceful, varied and enchanting, small but approachable, butterflies lead you to the sunny side of life, and everyone deserves a little sunshine. *~Jeffrey Glassberg*

As the Lord had finished creating the earth, something was missing, so He chose pieces from all the flowers, threw them into the sky and blew life into them, and the butterflies were born.

Therefore if any man is in Christ, he is a new creature; old things have passed away; behold, all things have become new. *~2 Corinthians 5:17 NKJV*

Life Lessons from a Butterfly~Let go of the past. Trust the future. Embrace change. Come out of the cocoon. Unfurl your wings. Dare to get off the ground. Ride the breezes. Savor the flowers. Put on your brightest colors. Let your beauty show. *~Unknown*

We delight in the beauty of the butterfly, but rarely admit the changes it has gone through to achieve that beauty. *~Maya Angelou*

How does one become a butterfly? You must want to fly so much that you are willing to give up being a caterpillar. *~Trina Paulus*

Love is like a butterfly—it goes through many changes before it becomes a thing of beauty.
                                                     ~Unknown

You will need:
• live butterflies in boxes

Cambodian Cord

Red Thread of Fate

(Asian)

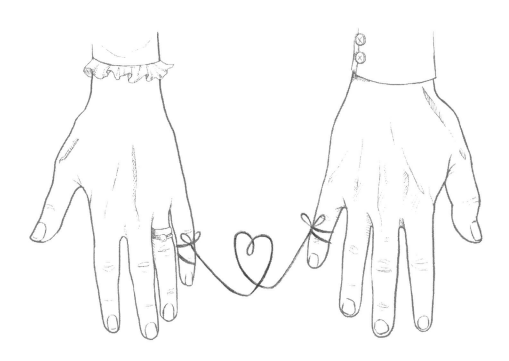

CAMBODIAN CORD *(Red Thread of Fate~Asian)*

(Officiant): In Asia, the color red is a sacred color and signifies great joy and celebration. There is an ancient Cambodian fable that says couples who are destined to be together are joined to one another at birth by an invisible red cord—the "Cambodian Cord." As time goes by and the two grow up, the invisible red cord begins to shrink in length. Each passing year, the cord gets shorter and shorter, so when the moment comes for the couple who is destined by fate to meet, the cord has shrunk so much, the two soulmates are standing face to face.

Cambodian Cord Procedure

(Officiant): At this time, I will take the red cord and tie a knot in the middle of it. Then I will offer a blessing for **Groom** and **Bride** and their marriage.

(Officiant takes a long red cord and ties a knot in middle of it as he makes a wish or offers an Asian blessing for Bride and Groom and their marriage.)

(Officiant): **Groom** and **Bride**, a wish for the two of you...
May you respect each other like honored guests. May you always see heart to heart as reflections of each other. May fragrant flowers bloom and a full moon shine over your life together. And may your joy and happiness be forevermore.

Now I will pass the cord to family and friends, and ask each of you to offer a silent blessing or wish for the Bride and Groom as you tie a knot in the red cord. Then continue to pass the cord so everyone may offer their blessings and good wishes symbolized by the many knots tied in the red cord.

(Red cord is passed first to immediate family, then friends. They say a silent prayer or make a wish for couple and tie a knot in cord at end of their prayer.)
- *Parents offer their silent prayers or wishes and tie their knots first, followed by siblings who offer their silent prayers or wishes and tie their knots*
- *Cord then may be passed through bridal party who offer their prayers or wishes and tie their knots*
- *When last person has tied a knot, cord is given back to Officiant*
- *Officiant may either tie ends of thread to Bride's and Groom's pinky fingers, or drape cord over Bride's shoulders or neck and offers a final blessing*

(Officiant): **Groom** and **Bride**, as you look at this red cord and all the many knots that have been tied in it, may it forever remind you of all the loving blessings and good wishes made for you by your families and friends on this, your wedding day.

Note: Some couples choose to tie a red thread joining their pinky fingers throughout the ceremony, representing their fated destiny of being soul mates forever. Others choose to have the knotted red thread draped over the Bride's shoulders.

You will need:
- red embroidery thread or red string

Circle Of Love

(Nature-inspired border of blessings)

CIRCLE OF LOVE *(Nature-inspired border of blessings)*

Circle of Love~*Version 1*

This nature-inspired ritual is a wonderful way to include all your guests in the wedding. A circle is formed around the ceremony site with either a garland of greenery, a piece of rope, a string or ribbon, creating a "Circle of Love." When the guests arrive, they are invited to collect a small piece of nature (flower petals, seashells, shiny crystals or smooth stones) from bowls placed at the entrance. Before being seated, the guests hold their item and make a wish or offer a blessing for the couple, then place it upon the circle, creating a sacred place for the ceremony.

Since everyone participates in the ritual, it helps them to feel a part of the marriage and denotes a sense of community and family.

(Guests choose object of nature, say a blessing or make a wish, and place nature piece on circle.)

(After Bride and Groom enter Circle of Love, Officiant explains its meaning.)

(Officiant): You will notice that **Groom** and **Bride** have chosen to say their wedding vows inside a circle—a "Circle of Love." We know a circle has no beginning and no end; it is never-ending, just like their love is never-ending. So it is very fitting for them to be married inside a circle.

But they also wanted to include you in their Circle of Love, and that is why you were asked to contribute something to the circle when you arrived. They consider you to be "family" and want to share their love with all of you, just as you have shared your best wishes and blessings for them when you placed your object of nature on the circle.

The Bride and Groom will collect these articles of nature, reminding them of God's handiwork, and keep them as mementos of all the love, blessings and good wishes they received today from you, their extended family.

The family is a circle of strength and love. With every birth and every union, the circle grows. Every joy shared adds more love to the circle. Every crisis faced together makes the circle stronger. Family is where life begins and love never ends. May you always be included in this Circle of Love.

You will need:
- garland, rope, string or ribbon
- flowers, greenery, seashells, crystals, stones

Heart of Love~*Version 2*

A garland of greenery is fashioned into the shape of a heart before the ceremony begins. When guests arrive, they each are given a flower, such as a gardenia blossom (or whatever flower the Bride has chosen). As they walk down the aisle, they make a wish or say a prayer for the couple and place the flower onto the heart-shaped garland—the "Heart of Love."

A sense of community is created with the participation of the guests, making everyone feel included in the wedding ceremony.

(Guests choose flower, make a wish or say a prayer, and place it on heart-shaped garland.)

(After Bride and Groom enter Heart of Love, Officiant explains its meaning.)

(Officiant): Love is in the air and our hearts are filled with joy for **Groom** and **Bride.** Today, they have chosen to give their promises of love inside a heart, because they know that what is *inside* the heart is what truly matters. So this "Heart of Love" that surrounds them encompasses all the feelings they have for each other, as well as the feelings of affection they have for each one of you.

God gave us eyes to see the beauty in nature, but he gave us hearts to see the beauty in each other. **Groom** and **Bride** have found that beauty in one another, and have fallen deeply in love with each other's hearts.

It is said that we come to love not by finding a perfect person, but by learning to see an imperfect person perfectly. And we can only do that when we look at someone through the eyes of the heart.

They say "love is blind." Love is not blind. It sees more, not less. But because it sees more, it is willing to see less. The heart forgives all the little imperfections of our character. It is a heart full of love that overlooks these imperfections and sees the true essence of its beloved.

Because each of you contributed to this Heart of Love when you made your wish and placed your flower in the garland, the Bride and Groom will exchange their vows in the collective love and blessings of their family and friends. There is no greater gift you can give them than your love and support. It is this gift that will help them grow in their wondrous love for one another throughout their lives together. It is their wish that you will open your hearts to them always as you do today, and share in their journey as they learn to look at life through the eyes of the heart—the Heart of Love.

You will need:
• garland, rope, string or ribbon
• flowers and greenery

Crowning Ceremony

(Greek Orthodox)

CROWNING CEREMONY *(Greek Orthodox)*

There is much symbolism in a Greek Orthodox wedding ceremony, and most brides who wish to include all those traditions will be married in a Greek Orthodox Church by a priest. However, many brides with this heritage, who choose to marry outside the church, still wish to include the "Crowning Ceremony," a beautiful, symbolic tradition.

This is a Greek Orthodox tradition where crowns or small wreaths, tied with white ribbon are placed on the Bride's and Groom's heads by the priest or wedding officiant.

The crowns symbolize the glory God gives them as newlyweds, now established as the King and Queen of their home, which they will rule with wisdom, justice and integrity.

The crowns are joined with a white ribbon, signifying the unity of the couple and the presence of Christ who unites them and blesses their marriage.

Their religious sponsor, the Koumbaro or Koumbara, exchanges the crowns over their heads three times, symbolizing the Holy Trinity—the Father, the Son and the Holy Spirit.

(Crowns are brought to altar.)

(Officiant): Bless these crowns *(sign of the cross)* as the Bride and Groom are crowned unto one another. The servant of God, **Groom**, is crowned for the servant of God, **Bride**, in the name of the Father, the Son and the Holy Spirit. The servant of God, **Bride**, is crowned for the servant of God, **Groom**, in the name of the Father, the Son and the Holy Spirit.

(Officiant or Koumbaro/Koumbara places crowns on Bride's and Groom's heads.)

(Officiant): O, Lord our God, crown them with Glory and Honor.

(Koumbaro/Koumbara exchanges crowns three times. Crowns are left on for remainder of service and are removed after Kiss and before Presentation.)

Order of Greek Orthodox Wedding Ceremony

- Welcome
- Prayer
- Blessing of the Rings
- Ring Exchange
- Prayer
- Readings
- Lighting of Candles

- Binding of Hands
- Prayer
- Blessing of Crowns
- Crowning Ceremony
- Readings
- Common Cup
- Dance of Isaiah

- Lord's Prayer
- Pronouncement
- Kiss
- Removal of Crowns
- Presentation
- Recessional

You will need:
- two crowns or wreaths joined by white ribbon for Bride's and Groom's heads

Dove Release

DOVE RELEASE

(Officiant): **Groom** and **Bride** have elected to symbolize their lifelong commitment to their marriage with a "Dove Release." Doves are a perfect choice for this symbolic moment since they are recognized around the world to represent peace, love and harmony.

Doves also are known to mate for life. **Groom** and **Bride,** may this pair of doves, who bond together for life, serve as an inspiration as you both go forth, traveling a path started by two and joining as one with a never-ending love for one another.

As a symbolic gesture of setting off on their life together in harmony, **Groom** and **Bride** are going to release these two white doves. The doves will fly upward and circle above us a few times, then fly home together as a pair. As we watch these beautiful creatures soar up into the sky and then navigate their way back home, this too, is symbolic for today's marriage. Since we have just witnessed **Groom** and **Bride** make their promises to commit to each other for life, we also witness them beginning to soar toward their new life and home together.

Groom and **Bride,** may your marriage carry with it all the wonderful qualities the white dove represents—peace, love, harmony and faithfulness.

You may now release the white doves and give your love wings!

(Doves are released by Bride and Groom. They circle and then fly back home.)

Dove Readings *(optional)*

Two Doves
Two doves meeting in the sky
Two loves hand in hand, eye to eye
Two parts of a loving whole
Two hearts and a single soul

Two stars shining big and bright
Two fires bringing warmth and light
Two songs played in perfect tune
Two flowers growing into bloom

Two doves gliding in the air
Two loves free without a care
Two parts of a loving whole
Two hearts and a single soul
~*Unknown*

The Legend of the Dove

Once the Lord of Heaven chose two doves, both young and fair,
and told them of a very special journey they would share.
Go now upon the earth and seek two hearts where you may dwell,
and there I shall surely come and make my home with you as well.
We'll join the two and make them one, a husband and a wife,
my Spirit will endow their love with everlasting life.
Today the doves still bring the sacred promise from above,
to those whose hearts are open to the miracle of love.

~Native American Legend

On Wings of Doves

On the wings of these white doves,
our hopes and dreams will fly.
Join together, head for home,
sail across the sky.

~Unknown

Winged Flight

From today, this winged love begins its flight across the skies of time. It will fly above the bounds of earth and beyond the edge of now. For when hearts and minds come together as one, the union takes mere mortals to places never been. The flight of love will allow you to challenge your wildest dreams. Side by side you will explore the endless possibilities of your shared world. And your journey will soar and fly with bearings sound and direction true. May your winds be favorable and your skies remain clear as you guide your shared flight toward the rising sun. For in the dawn of each new day, you will find the light to guide your way. May you enjoy your journey along the way, and may you feel the gentle guiding presence of others who share the skies with you—the place of freedom, adventure and endless hope.

~Unknown

On Wings of Love

These white birds are a symbol of
a public confession of true love.
Spreading news for all to see,
this marriage is made of Peace, Harmony and Unity.
White winged messengers set free today
are sent with blessings that will never fade away.

~Unknown

You will need:

• two white doves
• cage to hold doves (may be decorated)

Family Vows

(Participation of children in ceremony)

FAMILY VOWS *(Participation of children in ceremony)*

Celebration of the New Family

(Officiant): When a couple marries, it is not just the joining of two lives together, it is the coming together of families, as well. This is especially true today. For as **Groom** and **Bride** become husband and wife, they also are joined by **Child/ren** to become a family. At this time, we want to recognize this child/these children and acknowledge his/her/their importance on this wedding day.

Commitment to the Children

(Children come forward and form a circle or semi-circle with Bride and Groom. They may all join hands as Bride and Groom read following vows to children.)

Vow 1

(Groom and Bride): Today, as we become husband and wife, we welcome you, **Child/ren,** into our new family. (or, Today, as we become husband and wife, we include you in this union, **Child/ren,** because you are a part of this family.) We recognize that you are a precious gift from God. We promise to be there for you always, to comfort you and care for you, to protect you and provide for you, to guide you and listen to you, and most of all, to love you with all of our hearts forever and ever.

Other Family Vows

Vow 2

(Officiant): Over some time now, the four (or other number) of you have gotten to know each other, sharing meals, hanging out and just spending time together. You have become the "fearsome foursome" (or other nickname) and successfully melded into a modern-day family. Your support for this marriage is very important to **Groom** and **Bride. Bride/Groom** is joining this family circle as your father's wife/mother's husband, but she/he also comes into this family as a friend who you kids can count on, and most of all, a woman/man who loves you very much.

Vow 3

(Officiant): **Groom** and **Bride**, you have declared your love for each other. In your decision to spend the rest of your lives together, you have accepted the responsibilities of parenthood toward each other's children from other important relationships. You have established a home where each child finds love, security and acceptance. As part of your love for each other, I ask you to make your promises to them. *(Choose or write family vows and say them to children here.)*

Vow 4

(Officiant): **Groom** and **Bride**, today as you make your vows to each other with the promise of love and companionship, will you also do the same for **Child/ren**? Will you promise to honor and respect him/her/them as (an) individual(s) and guide his/her/their growth and development? Will you pledge to cherish him/her/them, encourage him/her/them, and make your home a place where there is trust, love, friendship and laughter? Will you hold his/her/their hand(s) through his/her/their mistakes rather than preventing him/her/them from making them? Will you promise to show him/her/them how to find happiness rather than tell him/her/them? Will you make these promises to **Child/ren** lovingly and freely?
(Bride and Groom): Yes.

(Officiant): Will you do the same for any other children you may bring into the world as his/her/their siblings?
(Bride and Groom): Yes.

(Officiant): For those children who no longer live with you, will your door always be open for them?
(Bride and Groom): Yes.

(Officiant): **Groom and Bride**, you have just made your promises. Promise is a big word. It either makes something—or it breaks everything. And so, on this day, I ask you to honor and keep these promises you have made to this child/these children.

Vow 5

(Officiant): **Child/ren**, the Bride and Groom would like to make some special promises to you because you are very important to them. They also want to remind you that their commitment of love to each other opens up a whole new world of people who will become your family—people who will love you and care about you and help you find your way in the world. So, I will ask them to make these promises to you.

(Officiant): **Groom** and **Bride**, will you continue to love and support this child/these children? Will you take the time to listen to him/her/them, to cherish him/her/them and to guide him/her/them? Will you show him/her/them respect, kindness, tolerance and honesty? Acknowledging the past, will you respect the unseen ties that bind him/her/them? Will you provide a safe, caring and loving home where this/each child is encouraged to develop his/her/their own unique qualities, in the knowledge that he/she/they always will be loved and valued for himself/herself/themselves? Will you this day make these promises lovingly and freely?
(Bride and Groom): Yes, we promise.

Vow 6

(Groom or Bride): **Child/ren**, I want you to know how blessed I feel every day just knowing you. You are the energy that flows through my veins. You inspire me. I can't imagine the man/woman I would have become without you in my life. Thank you for accepting **Bride/Groom** into our world. Nobody knows more than you how she/he has been there for us. You are (an) amazing kid(s) and I am proud to call you my son(s)/daughter(s). I love you!

Vow 7

(Groom or Bride): **Child/ren**, I have known you a long time. You and your father/mother are the people who know me best in this world, the people I eat with every day, the first I see in the morning and the last I see at night. The two (or other number) of you are my strength and my world. We are a family, and I consider you to be (one of) the most important people in my life. I am so thankful you have allowed me to be a part of your life, too. I love you very much!

Vow 8

(Groom or Bride): **Child/ren**, thank you for sharing Daddy/Mommy with me, and for loving me and allowing me to love you with all my heart. I was not there when you took your first steps, but I promise I will love and support you in every step you take in your life from this day on.

Vow 9

(Groom or Bride): I love you, **Child/ren**. I am devoted to making your life full of happiness and accomplishments, nurturing your creativity, encouraging your independence, and making sure you always know what a gift you are to this world and to me.

Vow 10

(Groom or Bride): I love you, **Child/ren**. I am committed to meeting your needs and fulfilling your dreams. I will encourage you in all your accomplishments, help you to thrive to your fullest potential, and while you reach for the sky, keep you grounded by the love of our family and home.

Vow 11

(Officiant): **Child/ren**, I'd like to ask you to make some promises just like the Bride and Groom made promises to each other. So after each question, if you think you can make that promise, I'd like you to answer "yes." Do you promise to accept each other just as you are? Do you promise to try your best to be patient, kind, tolerant, respectful and accepting of each other's differences? Do you promise to work hard to settle any disagreements or arguments so your friendships can grow stronger? Do you promise to listen to your parents and do your best to obey them at all times? Do you promise to help each other when someone needs help? Do you promise to bring laughter to this home? Do you promise to always try to make your parents proud of the choices you make? And finally, do you promise to love each other with all your hearts to infinity and beyond?
(Children): Yes. We promise.

(Officiant): Remember, only make promises you can keep and keep every promise you make!

Vow 12

(Groom or Bride): Today as I marry your mother/father, you become my family. I am so glad you are my family now because I love you so very much. I promise I will take care of you always and do my very best to make you happy. But most of all, I promise to love you forever—no matter what. Thank you for letting me share my life with you and your mom/dad.

Home and Family Blessings

Blessing 1

(Officiant): I ask that your home be a place of happiness and joy for all who enter it. May it be a place where the old and the young are renewed in each others' company. May your home be a place for growing and sharing, a place for music and celebration, a place for laughter and tears, a place where you feel safe to express any emotion you may feel. May your home be a place of refuge where every one of you can find the comfort of always knowing that you will be accepted and loved unconditionally.

Blessing 2

(Officiant): May God bless your marriage and family as you create a new home together. A family is a circle of strength and love. With every birth and every union, the circle grows. May every joy shared add love to the circle, and may every crisis faced together make the circle even stronger. May your family become like a beautiful rainbow as each color of your lives is carefully blended together with both the showers and the sunshine of God's love. Amen.

Blessing 3

(Officiant): Lord, you have created the family to be a place where people can experience love, learn important life lessons, and find unequaled encouragement. May your perfect design be reflected in this new family. I pray you would unite and bind this family together, and even in togetherness, may they allow space to be individuals. Help each person to love, respect and encourage others within the family. May the care and kindness they show to each other also be extended to those outside the family, that others might see your presence through them. Amen.

Family Readings (optional)

Family is Forever

A family is made of love and tears, laughter and years.
It grows stronger with the passing of time,
    more precious with the making of memories.
Sometimes a family is made of ones you don't like for a while...
    but you love for a lifetime.
It's a gift whose value is found not in numbers
    but in its capacity to love.
It's the place you find someone
    to encourage you, believe in you, celebrate with you and comfort you.
A family is where your heart feels most at home because you're
    always wanted, always welcomed, always needed, always loved. *~Crystal-Lynn Barringer*

A Family

A family is a place where you can cry and laugh,
and be silly, or sad, or cross,
where you can ask for help,
and tease and yell at each other,
and know that you will always be loved.

A family is made up of people who care about you when you are sad,
who love you all the time, no matter what, and who share your good times.
They don't expect you to be perfect,
but just want you to try to be the best you can be.

A family is a safe place like a circle,
where we learn to like ourselves,
where we learn about making good choices,
where we learn to think about things before we do them,
where we learn to be honest, and to have manners and respect for other people,
where we are special,
where we share ideas,
where we listen to them and they listen to us,
where we learn the rules of life to prepare ourselves for the world.

The world is a place where anything can happen.
If we grow up in a loving family like our family, we are ready for the world. *~Unknown*

Family

A family gives you unconditional love,
    strength and guidance they get from above.
They listen when you need an ear,
    and one thing is, they always care.
When you need a hand, they'll lend you theirs;
    if you're crying, they will wipe your tears.
If you need comfort, you know where to go;
    their love is never hidden, it is always shown.
They always boast about you to anyone they meet—
    family, friends and even strangers on the street.
A family is precious and kind;
    a family is truly divine.
A family is God's gift to everyone;
    they are what make your house your home.
To be appreciated you don't have to go far,
    because your family loves you for who you are. ~*LaTisha Parkinson*

They Are a Family, Uniquely Combined

As they enter the room with spirits entwined,
    they are a family, uniquely combined.
The warmth they share seems to fill them with pride;
    they are a family, they stand side by side.
It doesn't just happen spontaneously,
    this family so close, emotionally.
They live and they love, always showing they care,
    through good times and bad, together they share.
And now at this time, so happily rejoicing,
    expressing so clearly the love they're endorsing.
They stand as a family and always shall be
    like links on a chain, like leaves on a tree,
Connected by feelings of love they all know,
    filled with trust and respect, through the years as they grow. ~*Unknown*

Family~A Bond You'll Always Share

There's a certain kind of closeness that only families know.
    It begins with childhood trust and increases as you grow.
It's a very special feeling to know your family's there.
    It's a tie you can rely on, a bond you'll always share.
As a member of this family, we know that we belong.
    We're proud to say we're family, together we are strong.
Of all the blessings we may have, our Family means the most,
    And whether we live near or far, that bond will keep us close. ~*Glenda Campbell*

Our Family is Forever

Our family is like a patchwork quilt with kindness gently sewn,
  Each piece an original with beauty all its own.
With threads of warmth and happiness, it's lightly stitched together
  To last in love throughout the years—Our family is forever. ~*Unknown*

Our Family

United by the sorrows and joys that bind us, we are One.
One family, riding the roller-coaster of life, surviving the ups and downs with "relative sanity," never really knowing what's around the bend.
One family, sharing our space, our opinions, our hopes, our dreams, our fears and our disappointments. Cheering each other on through the best of times, and putting up with the worst in each other.
One family, through thick and thin, remaining steadfast and true, loving each other the way that families do, with the kind of love that grows stronger every day, even in the face of adversity, the kind of love that is, and always will be—forever! ~*Margaret Graveline*

You will need:

• family vows written on note cards (if you will be saying vows to children)

Hand Washing

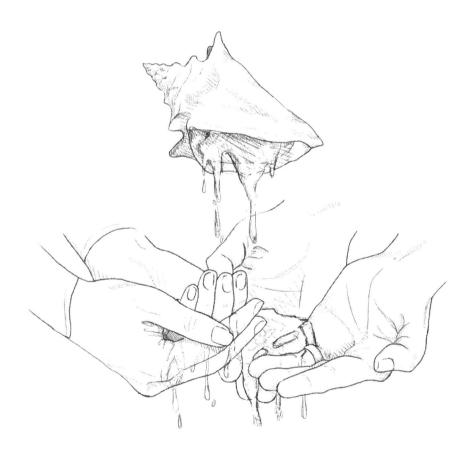

HAND WASHING

Hand Washing~*Version 1*

(Officiant): In the Hawaiian tradition, whenever a significant spiritual passage in life is made, you are called to "hiuwai." This transition is honored by a ritual cleansing of your spirit in a sacred body of water. Today, as you step over the threshold into the realm of marriage, your spirits will be cleansed and your hearts opened, ready to accept each other unconditionally and completely. We will demonstrate this with a "Hand Washing" ceremony. *(If ocean water is used, you may wish to add the following.)* In this ceremony, we will use ocean water as it has always been used for purification and bringing lives and souls into balance, as your lives are influenced and linked with the tides of the sea.

(Officiant pours water from koa bowl, pitcher or shell onto Bride's and Groom's hands individually for them to wash their own hands.)

(Officiant): **Groom** and **Bride**, the washing of your hands most importantly represents a complete and utter forgiveness of yourselves. By recognizing all that you have gone through and grown into, you are able to stand here today with the depth, capacity, abilities and compassion to love one another as deeply as you do. Therefore, from this day forward, your lives together are made anew, and nothing in your past can or will be held against you. All disagreements, conflicts and hurts are pardoned. You now enter into your union totally forgiven.

(Officiant pours water onto Bride's and Groom's hands so they may wash each other's hands.)

(Officiant): **Groom** and **Bride**, I will ask you to wash each other's hands as a promise that, throughout your lives and marriage, you will continue to find it in your hearts to forgive one another, no matter what arises. The Bible says, "Be kind to one another, tender-hearted, forgiving each other, just as God in Christ also has forgiven you" *(Ephesians 4:32 NASB)*. At this time, I ask you to recognize that forgiveness is a vital conduit for your love to flow through. Mother Theresa once said, "If we really want to love, we must learn how to forgive."

(Bride and Groom wash each other's hands.)

(Officiant): Now you may dry each other's hands with the tenderness you will show each other throughout your lives. And may you always forgive one another so your love may flow freely between the two of you each and every day of your lives together. Remember, there is no love without forgiveness, and there is no forgiveness without love.

(Bride and Groom dry each other's hands with small hand towel or cloth.)

Hand Washing~*Version 2*

(Bride and Groom approach table set up with hand towels and glass bowl of water. Flowers or lemon slices floating in water is a nice touch.)

(Officiant): **Groom** and **Bride**, today, in front of your family and friends, you begin your life together as a married couple. As with any new endeavor, it is best to start with a clean slate, putting problems big and small behind you. You come acknowledging that the person you have chosen is not perfect, yet fits with you in a way no other person can. Whatever difficulties you may have experienced, today you have decided your love is bigger than any of them, and you have chosen a life together.

Water brings forgiveness and we all need forgiveness. We need to forgive others and we need to forgive ourselves. There is no love without forgiveness, and there is no forgiveness without love. Mother Teresa once said, "If we really want to love, we must learn how to forgive."

This act of forgiveness now will be demonstrated with a "Hand Washing" ceremony. As you wash your hands in this bowl of water, forgive yourself and forgive each other for any pain in the past. Allow yourself to be forgiven for your human imperfections.

(Couple washes their own hands.)

(Officiant): Allowing yourselves to have your hands dried by each other signifies your vulnerability. We have to be vulnerable; it breaks through isolation. And in our own vulnerability, we become more caring and understanding of our partner. In a loving and compassionate marriage, to achieve the greatest intimacy, you must have the courage to be open and vulnerable to each other. Being open is the only way to allow your heart to feel true pleasure. Love isn't really love until it becomes vulnerable.

(Couple dries one another's hands.)

(Officiant): Do you begin your lives together with grace, compassion, openness and forgiveness?

(Couple): We do.

(Officiant): Then as your marriage grows, may you continue to show love and forgiveness to one another throughout your life together.

You will need:
- bowl or pitcher of water (may use shell to hold water instead)
- flowers or lemon slices to float in water bowl *(optional)*
- two small hand towels or cloths

Handfasting

(Celtic)

HANDFASTING *(Celtic)*

(Officiant): Have you ever wondered where the words "tying the knot" come from? The expression "tying the knot" refers to the traditional Celtic marriage ritual of "Handfasting." "Handfasting" is an ancient Celtic word for wedding, and was recognized as a binding contract of marriage between a man and woman before weddings became a legal function of the government or a responsibility of the church.

After the wedding vows and ring exchange, the couple's hands were bound together with a cord that was tied in a "love knot," signifying the joining of their lives in a sacred union. Today, Handfasting is a symbolic ceremony to honor a couple's desire for commitment to each other, and to acknowledge their lives and their destinies are now bound together.

Groom and **Bride**, please join your hands, and with your hands, your hearts. As you clasp hands and cross them, they form an eternity symbol, which illustrates your eternal love for one another.

(Couple joins both hands and then cross them, creating an eternity symbol.)

(Officiant holds up handfasting cord and addresses couple.)

(Officiant): **Groom** and **Bride**, this cord is a symbol of the life you have chosen to live together. Up until this moment you have been separate in thought, word and deed. But as this cord is tied together, so shall your lives become intertwined. With this cord, I bind you to the vows you have made to one another. With this knot, I tie you heart to heart, together as one.

(Officiant wraps cord loosely around Bride's and Groom's wrists to tie a "love knot.")

(Officiant): **Groom** and **Bride**, the "love knot" created by this binding is not bound by the cord, but instead, by your own vows of love. For, as always, you hold in your hands the making or breaking of this union.

May this "love knot" always be a reminder of the binding together of your two hands, two hearts and two souls into one. And so are you bound, each to the other, for all the days of your lives.

(Cord then may be removed. Many couples choose to keep "love knot" as a memento of their union.)

Note: The Handfasting tradition coordinates well with the Blessing of the Hands tradition. *(See Blessing of the Hands, page 15.)*

You will need:
- handfasting cord made of ribbon, rope, cord, leather strip, pearls, charms (may be found online or craft your own)

Holy Communion

The Lord's Supper~Holy Eucharist

HOLY COMMUNION *(The Lord's Supper~Holy Eucharist)*

Explanation of Communion

(Couple may choose to kneel or stand during Communion.)

(Officiant): **Groom** and **Bride**, you have chosen to partake in "Holy Communion" today. Communion is taken to commemorate that Christ died on the cross for the salvation of all mankind, including the two of you. Because of your faith in Jesus Christ and your love for him, you choose to honor him today in this way, through Holy Communion, recognizing that he is the one who brought you together.

Communion Elements

(Officiant): Let us pray. Lord Jesus, in memory of your death and resurrection, we offer this life-giving bread, which represents your body, and this soul-saving cup, which represents your blood. Because of your death on the cross, all our sins have been forgiven. Thank you, Lord, for loving us so much that you would give your life for us in order that we may have eternal life with you. In the name of Jesus Christ I pray, amen.

Before Jesus was given up to death, a death he freely accepted, he took the bread and gave thanks. Then he broke it and gave it to his disciples saying, "Take, eat. This is my body which is broken for you. Do this in remembrance of me" *(1 Corinthians 11:24 NKJV).*

(Officiant offers plate with bread to Groom and Bride; then together they eat bread. Plate is placed on table provided.)

(Officiant): After supper, in the same way, Jesus took the cup and gave thanks, saying, "This cup is the new covenant in my blood, which is poured out for many [so that your sins may be forgiven]. Do this, as often as you drink it, in remembrance of me" *(Luke 22:20 NIV; Matthew 26:28 NIV; 1 Corinthians 11:25 NASB).*

(Officiant gives cup to Groom first; he drinks, then gives cup back to Minister, who gives cup to Bride to drink. Cup is placed on table provided.)

(Officiant): Lord, may **Groom** and **Bride** be brought together in unity by the Holy Spirit. May they always love you as you have loved them, inspiring them to reach out in love to others. May they continue to serve you with open hearts and open hands all the days of their lives. Amen.

Note: Ask the Bride and Groom if they want to take Communion publicly so everyone may hear what is being said, or if they want to take it privately in the service just between the couple and the Officiant.

You will need:
- small table covered with white tablecloth
- bread or wafers
- wine or grape juice
- small plate for bread or wafers
- goblet or chalice for wine
- white cloth napkin

Honey Ceremony

(Persian/Christian)

HONEY CEREMONY *(Persian/Christian)*

Persian~Version 1

(Officiant): Honey is a symbol of the sweetness in life and the sweetness of love. And so, with this dish of honey, we proclaim this day as a day of great joy and celebration, a day to remember, a day filled with the sweetness of life and love.

We thank you, God, for creating this divine substance and ask you to bless it, even as you will bless this holy union.

The Bride and Groom now will share in the "Honey Ceremony."

(Groom dips his pinky finger into honey and touches Bride's tongue. Bride then dips her pinky finger into honey and touches Groom's tongue.)

(Officiant): **Groom** and **Bride**, as you share this honey together, so may you share your lives together in perfect love and devotion under God's guidance. May you find life's joys doubly gladdened, its bitterness sweetened, and all things blessed by time, companionship and love.

Christian~Version 2

(Bride and Groom hold two honey containers while Officiant explains meaning.)

(Officiant): The Bride and Groom have chosen to include the "Honey Ceremony" in their wedding today to remind them of the sweet love they have found in each other.

Groom and Bride, a lot of work goes into making a marriage. As you grow in your love, it will take work, like the hard work of honey bees. Honey bees never sleep, they are diligent and persistent, they are devoted to the hive and will sacrifice their lives to protect it.

We would do well to learn from them in our devotion, sacrifice and diligence to make the sweet choice of love in marriage. And just like honey, you each are a special creation. God created you as intricate beings, one-of-a-kind individuals. Psalm 139 says you are "fearfully and wonderfully made." You are two individuals with unique and special qualities, and today you are joining those qualities into one. The honey you hold is like your life, unique and special, and on this wedding day, you are giving your life to the one you love, just as you give this honey to your beloved now.

(Groom dips his pinky finger in honey and touches Bride's tongue. Bride then dips her pinky finger in honey and touches Groom's tongue.)

(Officiant): Life is the flower for which Love is the honey. By partaking in the Honey Ceremony, you have a sweet start to your new life together. The honey symbolizes the sweetness of life and the sweetness of love. May it also be a reminder to keep sweetness in your words, for the Bible says, "Pleasant words are like a honeycomb, sweet to the soul and healing to the bones" *(Proverbs 16:24 NASB).*

Honey Quotes

Pleasant words are like a honeycomb, sweet to the soul and healing to the bones.

~Proverbs 16:24 NASB

Life is the flower for which love is the honey.

~Victor Hugo

For bees, the flower is the fountain of life. For flowers, the bee is the messenger of love.

~Kahlil Gibran

A day without you as a friend is like a pot without a single drop of honey left inside.

~Winnie the Pooh

Home is where your honey is.*~Unknown*

Advice from a honey bee: Create a buzz. Sip life's sweet moments. Mind your own beeswax. Work together. Always find your way home. Stick close to your honey. Bee yourself!

~Unknown

You will need:
- honey in honey pot or container(s) to dip finger in
- napkins or wet wipes to clean fingers

Infinity Unity Bracelet

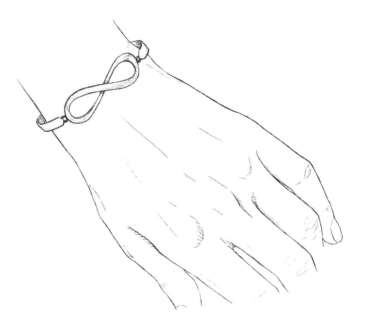

INFINITY UNITY BRACELET

The "Infinity Unity Bracelet" symbolizes the eternal love between a mother and child. Offering this symbolic piece of jewelry is a nice way to honor the mothers and make them feel special, and to acknowledge the moment that united their families as one.

(Officiant): Would the mothers of the Bride and Groom please come forward? The Bride and Groom would like to honor you with a special gift.

(Mothers come forward and stand between Bride and Groom next to their child.)

(Officiant): **Groom** and **Bride** would like to present their mothers with a special bracelet. It is called an "Infinity Unity Bracelet" because it is designed with an infinity symbol, which represents the eternal, unending love that exists between a mother and child.

The bond between mother and child is a special one. It remains unchanged by time or distance. It is the purest love of all—unconditional and true. It is understanding of any situation and forgiving of every mistake.

One of the most beautiful quotes I have ever heard about a mother's love was found in a note written by a mother to her child. It said this, "No one else will ever know the strength of my love for you. After all, you're the only one who knows what my heart sounds like from the inside. Love, Mom."

There is nothing more precious than the love a mother has for her child and the love a child has for his or her mother. It was a mother's kiss that first welcomed them into this world when they were born, and it is a mother's kiss that will welcome them into this new world of marital love.

Whenever **Groom's Mother** and **Bride's Mother** wear this bracelet, they not only will be reminded of this moment when their children became one, but also the moment that forever united their families as one. The Infinity Unity Bracelet then becomes a beautiful symbol of the everlasting love they share together.

(Bride and Groom present bracelets to mothers with hugs and kisses.)

Note: This ritual coordinates well with "A Mother's Kiss" ritual. You may find various styles of the Infinity Unity Bracelet online or in jewelry stores.

You will need:
• infinity unity bracelet (one for each mother)

90

Jumping The Broom

(African American)

JUMPING THE BROOM *(African American)*

The tradition of "Jumping the Broom" symbolizes sweeping away the old and welcoming the new —a symbol of new beginnings and the crossing of a threshold into a new life as husband and wife.

Jumping the Broom~Version 1

(Ceremony begins, oftentimes to the sound of the beating of traditional African drums, with guests forming a circle around Bride and Groom as they stand in front of broom on floor. Couple picks up broom and begins to sweep around in a circle while Officiant explains symbolism.)

(Officiant): "Jumping the Broom" may have its roots in an African tribal marriage ritual where sticks were placed on the ground, representing the couple's new home. However, it became popular among African American slaves who could not legally marry, so they created their own rituals to honor their unions. The broom was chosen because it has been the household symbol of "home" throughout history. It also has been said that the spray of the broom symbolizes the scattering of the African race throughout the world, and the broom handle represents the Almighty God, who holds them all together.

The Bride and Groom are sweeping together in a circle to signify the "sweeping away" of their former single lives, their past problems and their previous cares. The broom represents a threshold between past and present, and "jumping the broom" symbolizes the crossing of this threshold into a new relationship as husband and wife. Starting a new life with another person does require a "leap of faith," and by taking this leap, the couple shows their dedication to work together through all of life's circumstances, whatever they may be.

(Bride and Groom then place broom on floor and join hands as drums beat louder and faster. Everyone counts, "One, two, three…jump!" After they jump, Officiant may conclude ceremony with this version of a traditional slave poem.)

> Dark and stormy may come the weather,
> This man and woman are joined together.
> Let none but Him that makes the thunder,
> Put this man and woman asunder.
> I therefore announce you both the same,
> Be good, go long, and keep up your name.
> The broomstick's jumped, the world's not wide,
> She's now your own, go kiss your bride!

Sometimes a "double broom" is used instead, symbolizing the joining of two households into one.

(Officiant then would say): This double broom represents the two homes from which the Bride and Groom came, now joined together into one, symbolizing the new home created here this day.

This custom may take place during the ceremony after the couple is pronounced "husband and wife," or at the reception just after the bridal party enters the reception area.

Jumping the Broom ~ *Version 2*

A more simple version of "Jumping the Broom" (and probably more popular) takes place at the end of the wedding ceremony. Just before the Officiant introduces the couple as Mr. and Mrs., the broom is placed on the floor in front of them. They will hold hands and jump over the broom together, taking their first step as husband and wife over the threshold into their new married life.

(Officiant): In a moment, the Bride and Groom will "Jump the Broom," which symbolizes the crossing of a threshold into a new relationship as husband and wife. Starting a new life with another person does require a "leap of faith." So, after I present them as Mr. and Mrs., let's all count to three and say, "Jump!" as the newlyweds take that leap and jump over the broom into their new life together.

Ladies and gentlemen, it is my privilege to introduce to you for the very first time as husband and wife, **(Mr. and Mrs.) Newlywed.**

(Everyone counts, "One, two, three…jump!")

(Couple jumps over broom and exits.)

You will need:
- decorated broom (single or double); brooms are usually decorated with flowers, lace, ribbons, shells, charms or kente cloth

Lei~Garland Exchange

(Hawaiian / Indian)

96

LEI~GARLAND EXCHANGE *(Hawaiian/Indian)*

The Bride and Groom, and oftentimes family members, exchange leis (Hawaiian) or garlands (Indian), symbolizing the unbroken circle of love, respect, acceptance and commitment, along with the unity of the new family created from their marriage. Following are several versions.

Lei/Garland Exchange~Version 1
(Couple exchange only)
(No words spoken)

This exchange is performed at the beginning of the ceremony. The Best Man will hold the Groom's lei/garland for the Bride, and the Maid of Honor will hold the Bride's lei/garland for the Groom. When the Bride makes her entrance and meets her Groom at the front, they will take the leis/garlands from the Maid of Honor and Best Man and adorn each other with them.

Lei/Garland Exchange~Version 2
(Couple exchange only)
(Words spoken by Officiant and couple)

(Officiant): **Groom** and **Bride**, like a wedding ring, the flower lei/flower garland is an unbroken circle that symbolizes your eternal commitment and unending love for one another. The beauty of each individual flower is not lost when it becomes a part of the lei/garland, but rather, is enhanced because of the strength of its bond. Just as each of you are individuals, your coming together as one serves to enhance your beauty and strengthen the love that already was present in each of your hearts.

(Officiant): As a token of your love and deep desire to be forever united in heart and soul, **Groom**, you may place a lei/flower garland around your beloved.

(Groom places lei/garland on Bride and kisses her cheek.)

(Groom): **Bride**, please wear this lei/flower garland as a symbol of my never ending love. Aloha.

(Officiant): As a token of your love and deep desire to be forever united in heart and soul, **Bride**, you may place a lei/flower garland around your beloved.

(Bride places lei/garland on Groom and kisses his cheek.)

(Bride): **Groom**, please wear this lei/flower garland as a symbol of my never ending love. Aloha.

(Officiant): Just as these leis/flower garlands encircle each of you, may you always feel encircled by one another's love.

Lei/Garland Exchange~Version 3

(Acknowledgment of children)

(Bride and Groom present children with leis/garlands)

(Officiant): This moment in time is truly a cause for joyous celebration, for we are gathered here to witness not only the beginning of a new marriage, but also the beginning of a new family.

Groom and **Bride** would like to recognize the important role that **Child/ren** play(s) in this marriage celebrated today by presenting him/her/them with a symbolic gift of love—a lei/garland of flowers.

(Officiant to children): When this lei/flower garland is placed around you, it means you are forever a part of this family, just like each flower is a part of this lei/garland. The lei/flower garland is in the shape of a circle, and a family is also a circle—a circle of love.

(Bride and Groom adorn each child with lei/flower garland, say "I love you," then give them a hug and a kiss.)

(Officiant): Your family is now a circle of strength and love. With every birth and every union, the circle grows. May every joy shared add love to the circle, and may every crisis faced together make the circle even stronger. From this day forth, you will be more than just one couple. You will be a whole united family, drawn together by love and always held together by love.

Lei/Garland Exchange~Version 4

(Couple and parents/family exchange)

(Bride and Groom present parents/family with leis/garlands)

(Officiant): **Groom** and **Bride**, these leis/flower garlands symbolize the unbroken circle of love, respect, acceptance and commitment you are making to one another today. Please exchange your leis/flower garlands with each other at this time.

(Bride and Groom exchange their leis/flower garlands.)

(Officiant): Because of your union, your families are joining together as well. These leis/flower garlands represent the unity of the new family created from your marriage. Please show your acceptance of them and welcome each family member by placing a lei/garland around them.

(Bride and Groom place leis/garlands around family members and give each one a kiss on cheek. They also may say "Aloha" or "I love you.")

(Officiant): Just as these leis/garlands encircle each of you, may you always feel encircled by each other's love.

Lei/Garland Exchange~Version 5

(Uniting Bride's and Groom's families)

(Bride and Groom honor their parents and present them with leis/garlands)

(Officiant): **Groom** and **Bride**, today you stand before us ready to share the rest of your lives together as a married couple. But long before today, your parents provided you with a foundation of love that has brought you to this moment.

At this time, **Groom** and **Bride** would like to acknowledge the love and sacrifice their parents have made to make their children into who they are today—a man and a woman who are ready to be committed in a loving marriage of their own. They honor their parents with a symbolic gift of love, the giving of a flower lei/garland of flowers.

(Bride and Groom adorn parents with leis/flower garlands, kiss their cheeks and say, "I love you.")

(Officiant): **Groom** and **Bride**, may you provide your children with the same foundation of love as your parents gave to you.

Lei/Garland Exchange~Version 6

(Uniting families from different heritages)

(Mothers/Parents present Bride and Groom with leis/garlands, accepting each into their family)

(Officiant): **Groom** and **Bride** come here from two different families and two different heritages. We are especially grateful for the values and traditions that have flowed into them from those who have loved and nurtured them along life's way.

The heritage each brings to this marriage will continue to be an important element in their lives, but now will be shared between them. Out of these two families, a new family will be created, where they will pass on the best of these traditions to their children.

At this time, I will invite the mothers (or parents) to come forward to welcome their new family member by presenting them with a flower lei/garland of flowers.

(Officiant to mothers/parents): This lei/garland is a symbol of your blessings upon this marriage and the joining together of your families. Please welcome the Bride and Groom into your hearts and lives.

(Mothers/Parents put lei/garland around their new family member and give them a hug and a kiss.)

You will need:
• lei or flower garland for each person participating

Love Letters and Wine Box

LOVE LETTERS AND WINE BOX

(Officiant): **Groom** and **Bride** have chosen to include a unique ritual in their wedding today. It is called the "Love Letters and Wine Box" ceremony.

(Wine Box and Love Letters are lying on a table as Officiant explains meaning of ritual.)

(Officiant): This box contains a bottle of wine, two glasses, and a love letter from each to the other as they begin their marriage. The letters describe the good qualities they find in one another, the reasons they fell in love, and why they chose to marry. The letters are sealed in individual envelopes, and each has not seen what the other has written. They have created their very own romantic time capsule to be opened on their fifth wedding anniversary.

Groom and **Bride**, there is only one reason this box should be opened before your fifth anniversary. If ever there comes a time when you hit a bumpy road in your relationship and you are not seeing eye to eye, or you find your marriage enduring insurmountable hardships, let this box remind you of all the reasons you chose each other as your partner, and of all the things that helped shape the life you have created together.

Before you give up or make any irrational decisions, you are to open this box as a couple, sit and drink the wine together, and then read the letters you wrote to one another when you were united in marriage as husband and wife. By reading these love letters, you will reflect upon the reasons you fell in love and chose to marry each other here today.

Never take your blessings of being together for granted. The tender sentiments you wrote, your declaration of love, the reasons as to why you chose this person as your life partner will help put you back on even ground and, hopefully, give you enough reason to try again.

The hope is, however, that you will never have a reason to open this box until your fifth anniversary to celebrate and read your love letters. Then write new love letters to each other and place them back in the box with a new wine bottle to be opened on your tenth anniversary, continuing the tradition every five years for the rest of your lives. By doing this, you will have a romantic historical account of your life and love. I recommend that you keep the box prominently displayed in your home as a constant reminder of your love and commitment to each other.

Groom and **Bride**, may the cup of your lives be sweet as wine and full to running over with love. You may seal/lock the box.

(Minister, parents or other VIP can drive first nail, then Bride and Groom nail box shut. If you use a custom made wine box with a key, Bride and Groom both use key to lock box.)

You will need:
- decorative wine box, bottle of wine and bottle opener (box and bottle may be engraved)
- two wine glasses
- two love letters
- key to lock box, or nails and hammer to seal box

Love Locks

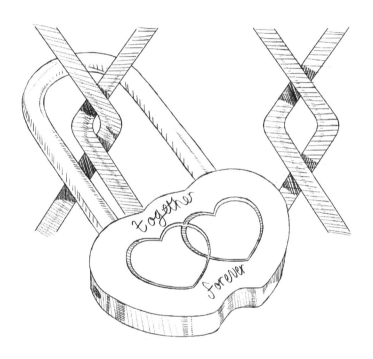

LOVE LOCKS

Love Locks~*Version 1*
(Couple using one lock)

(Officiant): We have just witnessed **Groom** and **Bride** declare their love and exchange their rings, symbolizing their lifelong commitment to each other. Now they wish to further symbolize the strengthening of their union with a new tradition—a "Love Locks" ceremony.

A lock and key can symbolize so much. For **Groom** and **Bride**, it represents the opening of their hearts to one another and the locking of the covenant that now binds them together in marriage.

Now, as you join your separate lives into one, I invite you to lock your Love Lock as a symbol of your commitment to one another. As you do, remember this lock is not like any other. Your Love Lock locks *one time only*! There is no key. This symbolizes your commitment to each other for all eternity. Your love is locked—*forever*!

(Bride and Groom lock their Love Lock to plaque, fence or other meaningful object.)

(Officiant): As this Love Lock will be locked forever, so it is with your hearts. The act of locking demonstrates that you are joined together in a lifelong partnership, a promise between you both that you will forever be one, with a oneness that will complement and complete you.

Groom and **Bride**, let this Love Lock remind you that, today, you have joined your lives, your hearts and your souls together—now, forever and always.

Note: This version uses only one lock, which is usually attached to an item like a metal tree, display plaque, gate, fence, bridge or another object chosen.
Love Locks and accessories may be found at **www.lovelocksonline.com**.

You will need:
- one padlock (may be engraved)
- display frame, plaque, hook found online *(optional)*

Love Locks~Version 2

(Couple using two locks)

(Officiant): We have just witnessed **Groom** and **Bride** declare their love and exchange their rings, symbolizing their lifelong commitment to each other. They wish to further symbolize the strengthening of their union with a new tradition—a "Love Locks" ceremony.

A lock and key can symbolize so much. For **Groom** and **Bride**, it represents the opening of their hearts to one another and the locking of the covenant that now binds them together in marriage.

Now, as you join your separate lives into one, I invite you to lock your Love Locks together as a symbol of your commitment to one another. As you do, remember these locks are not like any other. Your Love Lock locks *one time only*! There is no key. This symbolizes your commitment to each other for all eternity. Your love is locked—*forever*!

(Bride and Groom lock their Love Locks together.)

(Officiant): As these Love Locks will be locked together forever, so it is with your hearts. The act of locking demonstrates you are joined together in a lifelong partnership, a promise between you both that you will forever be one, with a oneness that will complement and complete you.

Groom and **Bride**, let these Love Locks remind you that, today, you have joined your lives, your hearts and your souls together—now, forever and always.

Note: This version uses two locks that lock together. They also may be locked to something else such as a gate, fence, bridge, hook or plaque.
Love Locks and accessories may be found at **www.lovelocksonline.com**.

You will need:
- two padlocks (may be engraved)
- display frame, plaque, hook found online *(optional)*

Love Locks~Version 3

(Family using many locks, one for each family member, to form a circle)

When children are blending into a family, the Groom, Bride and children may lock their individual locks onto each other's locks, forming a circle—a family circle.

(Officiant): **Groom**, **Bride** and **Child/ren**, today, you are officially becoming a family. Each one of you is a very important part of this family circle because it is not complete without you in it. As you combine with each other and complete each other as a family, you will link your lives and lock your hearts together, as symbolized by this "Love Locks" ceremony.

Now as you join your lives into one family, I will ask you to join your locks together as a symbol of your commitment to this family. Each of you will link your individual lock with each other's locks, which will form a circle. Your family also is a circle; it unites everyone within it, surrounds each one with love, protects those inside its boundaries, encompasses the hopes and dreams of those included in the family circle, and never, ever ends—family is forever.

(Each family member locks onto next person's lock, forming a circle when complete. Start with Bride, then children, end with Groom. Groom holds up circle of Love Locks while Officiant blesses family.)

(Officiant): May your family be a circle of love and strength, founded on faith, joined in love, kept by God, and locked forever together as one.

Note: This version uses many locks (one for each family member) to form a circle, representing the family circle forming this day.

Love Locks and accessories may be found at **www.lovelocksonline.com**.

You will need:
- padlocks for each family member (may be engraved)
- display frame, plaque, hook found online *(optional)*

Love Locks~*Version 4*
(Tree of Life Theme)

This "Love Locks" ceremony incorporates the "Tree of Life" theme. The following guide is used as you lock your first Love Locks to the Tree of Life, but may be customized for your family.

(Officiant): **Parents**, you have laid the foundation for **Groom's** and **Bride's** lives since the day of their birth. Through the years you implanted the seeds of love in their hearts and they became deeply rooted in that love. As you lock onto the roots of the Tree of Life, it represents strength and support. The message you engraved on your Love Lock is the commitment and joy you have shared with them and the blessings they have been to your lives.

(Parents lock their Love Locks onto roots of Tree of Life.)

(Officiant): **Groom** and **Bride**, today you join your separate lives together. The Love Lock you hold is a symbol of your commitment to one another. The message written upon your Love Lock is the promise of love, acceptance and unity (or whatever message you have chosen). The Love Locks Tree of Life represents all that you are and all that you will ever be, both as individuals and as a part of your union throughout your life together.

As you lock your Love Lock to the Tree of Life, remember the reason you have come here today. Your Love Lock locks *one time only*! There is no key. This symbolizes your commitment to each other for all eternity. Your love is locked—*forever*!

As your life unfolds in its many directions, the branches will bear its celebrations of life to come, and you will add Love Locks to those branches at that time in commemoration of that celebration. Today, you lock two hearts together; the love you share will be forever.

(Bride and Groom lock their Love Lock onto branches of Tree of Life.)

(If children are part of the union, the Love Locks Tree of Life Ceremony may include them also. Additional Love Locks may be engraved and locked to leaves on Tree of Life.)

(Officiant): We want to recognize **Child/ren**, who share(s) in this marriage and new family today. He/She/They will "lock his/her/their love" onto the branches of the Tree of Life. Every child is as individual and unique as a leaf on a tree. With love, compassion and patience, they will reach high and wide and become as strong as the roots, locking your family together forever as one.

(Children lock their Love Locks onto branches of Tree of Life.)

(After all love locks are locked onto Tree of Life, Officiant says):
And so it begins…Love…deeply rooted…always growing…and forever intertwined.

Note: Love Locks and accessories may be found at **www.lovelocksonline.com**.

You will need:
• Tree of Life plaque (found online)
• love locks for each participant

Love Locks Ceremony Readings (optional)

The Key to Love

The key to love is understanding,
    the ability to comprehend not only the spoken word
but those unspoken gestures,
    the little things that say so much by themselves.

The key to love is forgiveness,
    to accept each other's faults and pardon mistakes,
without forgetting, but with remembering
    what you learn from them.

The key to love is sharing,
    facing your good fortunes as well as the bad, together,
both conquering problems, forever searching for ways
    to intensify your happiness.

The key to love is giving,
    without thought of return,
but with the hope of just a simple smile,
    and by giving in but never giving up.

The key to love is respect,
    realizing that you are two separate people, with different ideas,
that you don't belong to each other,
    that you belong with each other, and share a mutual bond.

The key to love is inside us all.
    It takes time and patience to unlock all the ingredients
that will take you to its threshold.
    It is the continual learning process that demands a lot of work,
but the rewards are more than worth the effort,
    …and *that* is the key to love.

                                  ~Anon, 1st century China

Soulmate

A soulmate is someone who has locks that fit our keys and keys to fit our locks. When we feel safe enough to open the locks, our truest selves step out and we can be completely and honestly who we are. We can be loved for who we are and not for who we are pretending to be.

Each unveils the best part of the other. No matter what else goes wrong around us, with that one person we're safe in our own paradise. Our soulmate is someone who shares our deepest longings, our sense of direction. When we're two balloons, and together our direction is up, chances are we've found the right person. Our soulmate is the one who makes life come to life.
~*Richard David Bach, The Bridge Across Forever: A True Love Story*

The Key to My Heart

Late at night when I'm sound asleep,
    into my heart you softly creep.
I sit and wonder how it could be,
    but you must have stumbled across the key.
This key holds the secret to true love and more,
    so take it now and unlock the door.
And I pray that we will never part,
    now that you have the key to my heart.
~*Nicole C. Moore*

Quotes about Locks and Keys

Let me find the key to your heart so I can unlock your secret chambers of love. When I do find that key, I will lock myself in your heart forever. ~*Unknown*

We are two hearts locked together forever. ~*Unknown*

My heart to you is given,
    do give yours to me.
We'll lock them up together
    and throw away the key—forever. ~*Unknown*

Creative Ways to Incorporate Love Locks

- Love Locks may be engraved with names, dates, quotes, symbols or photos.

- Attach Love Locks to the Love Locks Tree of Life.

- Use Love Locks to secure a wedding time capsule box.

- Slide wedding rings onto a padlock for Ring Bearer to carry safely.

- Slide wedding rings onto a padlock to pass around for a Ring Warming ceremony.

- Bride and Groom each attach their wedding rings to a separate lock, then they unlock each other's rings, and as a couple, lock their two locks together.

- Bride and Groom attach their Love Locks to a gate, fence, bridge or tree at a romantic place while on their honeymoon, or in the town where they got married, or at another meaningful place to them.

- Bride, Groom and their children may lock their individual locks onto each other's locks, forming a circle—a family circle of strength and love.

- Couple may either toss the keys into a body of water, bury the keys, tie them to a balloon or melt them in a bonfire. Some couples choose to keep the keys and display them in a frame, or include them in a time capsule box, or attach them to a bracelet, necklace or locket as a keepsake.

Lucky Star

LUCKY STAR

(Officiant): Sometimes when two people meet, it's obvious that they are made for each other. Their love is "written in the stars" and just meant to be. The lovers walk around with "stars in their eyes" and seem to be "star struck." Do you see a theme here?

While **Groom** and **Bride** were planning their wedding, they decided to give each other a very special wedding gift, something lasting to symbolize their eternal love—a forever gift. I think they found the most lasting gift in the universe! They gave one another the gift of a star, a "Lucky Star," and they named the stars in honor of each other—one star, **Groom**, and the other star, **Bride**. They even have a certificate with the name of each star, the date it was dedicated (their wedding date), and a sky chart with the coordinates locating their two stars in the sky.

(Officiant may hold up certificate and sky chart to show guests.)

(Officiant): It has been said, "Each of us represents a star in the sky; sometimes we shine with the rest, sometimes we twinkle alone, and sometimes, when we least expect it, we fall and make someone's dreams come true." **Groom** and **Bride**, you are each other's "dream come true," and you both have found your "Lucky Star" in one another.

The two silver star ornaments **Groom** and **Bride** hold are symbols of the two stars named for them in the heavens. These ornaments have their names, wedding date and coordinates engraved on them. So on this, their wedding day, they wish to give their wedding gifts to each other as a symbol of their eternal love.

(As Groom and Bride exchange stars, they exchange words of love. Groom gives his star to Bride first and reads words of love, followed by Bride who gives her star and reads her words of love to Groom.)

(Groom): **Bride**, you are my "lucky star," because everything I've ever wished for is everything you are. I give you this star as a sign of my never-ending love.

(Bride): **Groom**, you are the flame in my heart, the light of my life, and the star in my night sky. I give you this star as a sign of my everlasting love.

(Officiant): I hope you will put your lucky stars in a place of honor in your home. Perhaps hang them on your Christmas tree each year to remind you that your love still shines, for love is the best gift of all.

As the song says, "When you wish upon a star, your dreams come true." Every time you look up into the night sky, you can "thank your lucky stars" you found each other, for that is the moment your dreams came true.

Groom and **Bride**—two stars from the same solar system, residing in the sky, together forever. May your love last as long as these stars will shine—forever and always, until the end of time.

Star Quotes

You are the flame in my heart, light of my life, star in my night sky. ~*Unknown*

You are my lucky star because everything I've ever wished for is everything you are. ~*Unknown*

A match can light up a fire, a star can light up the sky, but you are the only one who can light up my heart. ~*Unknown*

May the stars that watched you then, bless you always. ~*Unknown*

Let these stars bear witness to the love spoken between our hearts. ~*Unknown*

Each of us represents a star in the sky; sometimes we shine with the rest, sometimes we twinkle alone, and sometimes, when we least expect it, we fall and make someone's dreams come true.
~*Unknown*

Star light, star bright, first star I see tonight, I wish I may, I wish I might, have the wish I wish tonight.

When You Wish Upon A Star
When you wish upon a star
Makes no difference who you are
Anything your heart desires
Will come to you

If your heart is in your dreams
No request is too extreme
When you wish upon a star
As dreamers do

Fate is kind
She brings to those who love
The sweet fulfillment of
Their secret longing

Like a bolt out of the blue
Fate steps in and sees you through
When you wish upon a star
Your dreams come true ~*Ned Washington*

Note: You may choose only one star with your last name, wedding date and coordinates engraved, instead of two stars with first names engraved. Name a Star kit and Star Ornaments may be found at **www.starregistry.com**.

You will need:
• one or two star ornaments
• Name a Star kit

Marriage Box

Time Capsule

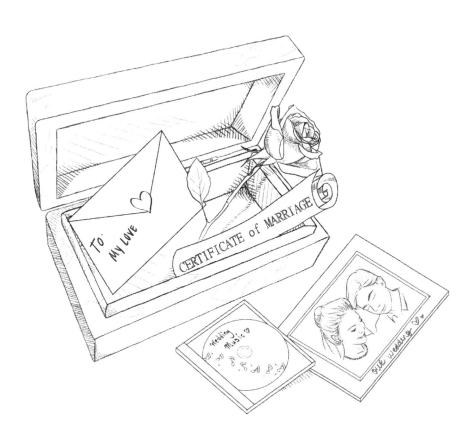

MARRIAGE BOX *(Time Capsule)*

The "Marriage Box" is a type of time capsule, but different from other time capsules in that the Bride and Groom will open it on each anniversary to add more memories to it. By doing this, you will have a recorded history of your marriage as it unfolds year by year.

Since you will be adding things every year, you will need a box large enough to hold these keepsakes for many years. You also may want to use dividers of some kind to identify each individual year. File cabinet dividers work well as you can write each year on the tab.

Each year, be sure to include a photo of you as a couple. Some couples choose to take a photo of themselves holding the previous year's photo. It's a fun way to see yourselves gradually growing old together. As Robert Browning said, "Grow old with me, the best is yet to be!"

It's a nice touch to write a love letter to your spouse each year, as well, to be read on the following anniversary. Take time to look through all the previous years of memories, as it will show you how much you have grown together. Some things may even surprise you.

Starting with your wedding day, you will put in memorabilia from your wedding.

Suggestions to include in Marriage Box from your Wedding Day:
- Wedding Photo
- Wedding Invitation
- Wedding Program
- Wedding Vows
- Marriage Certificate
- First Dance Song CD
- Wedding Video
- Pressed Flower from Bouquet
- Wedding Guest List or Love Notes from Guests
- Wedding Napkin or Matchbook
- Sealed Love Letter to Spouse

Suggestions to include in Marriage Box on your First Anniversary and following:
- Current Photo of You as a Couple
- Photos from Previous Year Together (current year photos of children, pets, new or remodeled house, car purchase, job change, awards earned, hobbies, trips, special events)
- New Sealed Love Letter to Spouse
- New Favorite Song or Movie
- Programs from Special Events
- Ticket Stubs
- List of Year's Highlights
- List of Dreams and Goals for Next Year

Marriage Box Ceremony

(Officiant): Today, **Groom** and **Bride** begin a new chapter in their journey of love together. They want to remember this moment forever. But, as time passes, we tend to forget things that once were important and precious to us. So, in order to remember this moment and all the moments yet to come in their marriage, they are going to create a "Marriage Box."

A Marriage Box is a type of time capsule that the Bride and Groom will open on each anniversary to add mementos of their previous year together. It may include things such as photos of them or of special people or pets, a list of important events from that year, ticket stubs, a CD of their current favorite song, a list of dreams and goals for the upcoming year, and a new sealed love letter to be read on the following anniversary. They will begin to fill the Marriage Box starting with items from this special day, their wedding day.

(Bride and Groom will place some initial items into Marriage Box, adding more later from their wedding day. Officiant may verbally identify each item as it is placed in box by couple so guests can enjoy knowing its contents.)

(Officiant): This Marriage Box will be full of prized, tangible mementos that represent precious, intangible moments—something you will cherish forever. But there are some other things you also must put into the Marriage Box if your marriage is going to flourish and grow, things you can not always see, but are felt in the heart.

Most people get married believing a myth that marriage is a beautiful box full of all the things they have longed for—companionship, intimacy, friendship and more. The truth is, marriage, at the start, is an empty box. You must put something in before you can take anything out. There is no love in marriage. Love is in people, and people put love in marriage. There is no romance in marriage. You have to infuse it into your marriage. A couple must learn the art and form the habit of giving, loving, serving, praising, keeping the box full. If you take out more than you put in, the box will be empty. *(J. Allan Petersen)*

Groom and **Bride**, each year as you continue to fill this box with treasures, souvenirs and keepsakes, remember to fill your marriage with respect, devotion and love.

Note: When choosing a box, you may use a metal or wooden one with lock and key, and decorate or engrave it to personalize it. You also may use a watertight plastic tote. Do not bury the box, as the contents easily can become damaged. Keep it in a cool, dry place or display it in your home.

You will need:
- large box (wooden or metal is best, but a watertight plastic tote also is fine)
- items from wedding day you may wish to include (photo, invitation, program, marriage certificate, vows, napkin, matchbook, first dance CD, wedding video, pressed flower, sealed love letter to spouse)

Marriage Vessel and the Rose

MARRIAGE VESSEL AND THE ROSE

The "Marriage Vessel and the Rose" ceremony may be used as an alternative to the Unity Candle, especially for outdoor weddings. You will need a table for the vessel and the rose. Filling the vessel with water is necessary only if you use the second version. The Officiant begins by explaining the significance of the ceremony.

(Officiant): To symbolize their ever-growing lifelong commitment to each other, **Groom** and **Bride** have chosen to share two gifts—the "Marriage Vessel and the Rose." The spiritual roots of the Marriage Vessel and the Rose grow out of an understanding of God as the Potter, or Creator of life *(holding up the vessel)*, and God as the Gardener, or Sustainer of life *(holding up the rose)*. The vessel of clay, lovingly shaped by the Potter, is a symbol of love's strength and endurance. Likewise, the rose, born of the tiniest of seeds, symbolizes the beauty and the potential of growing in love throughout life together. The miracle of the vessel is that it not only protects, but is enriched by that which it holds, the rose. Both the vessel and the rose are individually unique, yet when combined, they create an object of even greater beauty.

Marriage Vessel and the Rose~*Version 1*
(without water)

(Groom presents rose to Bride.)

(Groom): **Bride**, this rose represents the beauty I see in you./I thank you for the person you are/ and the person I am becoming because of your love for me.

(Bride presents vessel to Groom.)

(Bride): **Groom**, this vessel represents the strength I see in you./I thank you for the love and care you have given me,/and for all we will share together in this life.

(Bride places rose in vessel; then Bride and Groom hold it together.)

(Officiant): As your gifts bring beauty and purpose to each other, may your lives continue to enrich and strengthen one another.

Groom and **Bride**, as you share each passing day, and as your days become years, remember this tradition you have created. On each wedding anniversary, place one additional rose in the marriage vessel to symbolize your ever-growing love for one another. May the Marriage Vessel and the Rose always be a symbol of the beauty and strength you bring to each other's lives.

Marriage Vessel and the Rose~Version 2
(with water)

(Groom hands Bride a rose.)

(Groom): **Bride**, take this rose as a symbol of my love./It began as a tiny bud and blossomed,/ just as my love has grown for you.

(Bride places rose into vase filled with water.)

(Bride): **Groom**, I take this rose, a symbol of your love,/and I place it into water, a symbol of life./For just as this rose cannot survive without water,/I cannot live without you.

(Groom): In remembrance of this day,/I will give you a rose for each year on our anniversary/as a reaffirmation of my love/and the vows we have spoken here today.

(Bride): And I will refill this vessel with water each year on our anniversary,/ready to receive your gift of love/in reaffirmation of the new life you have given me/and the vows we have made to each other today.

(Bride and Groom join hands around rose-filled vessel.)

(Officiant): **Groom** and **Bride**, just as this rose and vessel of water give beauty and life to each other, so may your love blossom and grow throughout your life together.

Note: The Bride and Groom may write these words on note cards, or they may repeat them after the Officiant. If repeated, slashes in the text denote the breaks in the phrases.

You will need:
- vessel or vase (due to specific text, earthen or clay vessel is best, not glass or metal)
- rose
- water *(if using Version 2)*
- table to hold items

Memorial Moments

(Remembering loved ones)

MEMORIAL MOMENTS *(Remembering loved ones)*

Memorial Moments~Version 1

(Using flowers, candles or photos)

(Officiant): I would like to take a moment to acknowledge those l[...] with us today physically, but who are certainly with us in spirit…**Ho** *(Read names of honorees/loved ones and what relation they are to 1 Smith, father of Groom or Sue Jones, sister of Bride.)*

(If applicable, Officiant mentions flowers/candles/photos placed in their honor.)

(Officiant): These flowers/candles/photos have been placed here to honor his/her/their memory and the legacy of love he/she/they has/have left to his/her/their family/families. He/She/They occupies/occupy a very special place in our hearts and specifically the hearts of **Groom** and **Bride** who love him/her/them and miss him/her/them deeply.

Even though we can not see him/her/them here in this place, I believe he/she/they gives/give his/her/their blessing and is/are watching this celebration from the best seat in the house.

Memorial Moments~Version 2

(Special place in hearts)

(Officiant): We want to welcome you here today as **Groom** and **Bride** commit themselves to each other in marriage. We also want to remember **Honoree(s)**. Though he/she/they is/are not present today, he/she/they occupies/occupy a very special place in our hearts on this joyous day of celebration.

Memorial Moments~Version 3

(Here in spirit)

(Officiant): During our time together today, we would be remiss if we did not take a moment to honor and to remember a/some very special family member(s) who is/are not here in person, but who is/are very much here in spirit…**Honoree(s)**. We love him/her/them and miss him/her/them so much. We know he/she/they would be here if only he/she/they could be, to share your love and joy as you celebrate the happiest day of your life.

Memorial Moments~Version 4

(Moment of silence~Blow a kiss)

(Officiant): At this time, I would like to have a moment of silence in remembrance of **Honoree(s)**. Afterward, **Designated Individual** will count to three, and we all will blow a kiss into the air as an expression of our love.

Memorial Moments~*Version 5*

(Recent loss of loved one~Sorrow and Joy)

(Officiant): Today most likely will be an emotional time for many present here, both of sorrow and joy. Please be assured that it is not disrespectful to **Honoree(s)** to celebrate this wedding day. Neither is it disrespectful to our newlyweds to show your sorrow. It is appropriate to express all the emotions. Experiencing both laughter and tears, both sorrow and joy, are not only ok, but are very much a natural part of life. While we keep **Honoree(s)** in our hearts, we also celebrate the love of **Groom** and **Bride** and the new life they begin today as husband and wife.

Memorial Moments~*Version 6*

(Using crystals)

(Officiant): On this special day, **Groom** and **Bride** have chosen to honor their loved ones who are no longer with us. The crystals on the candelabra represent the love and light each of these special people brought into our lives. Though we can not see them, we know they are here; though we cannot touch them, we feel their presence and the warmth of their smiles. Their influence will forever illuminate our pathway, and the light of their love will be with us always.

You will need:
- photo of loved one(s)
- candles and lighter
- flowers and vase
- crystals and candelabra *(Version 6)*
- table to hold items

Message in a Bottle

(Beach Weddings)

MESSAGE IN A BOTTLE *(Beach weddings)*

(Officiant): **Groom** and **Bride** have chosen to include a very unique ritual during their ceremony today. They are going to throw into the sea a "Message in a Bottle."

Groom and **Bride** have collaborated together to write a love letter, not your typical love letter, but one with a special purpose. Within the letter, they have shared a little about themselves, how they fell in love, what they love about each other and their relationship, and most importantly, what they hope to gain from sending out this message in a bottle. Lastly, **Groom** and **Bride** have included a request for whoever finds the bottle to contact them upon reading their message and respond with their own life experience, along with a bit of marital or life advice.

The letter is placed in this bottle and sealed, and the bottle is to be thrown out to sea. Two identical copies of this letter have been created and sealed in a clear bottle so the couple can display it in their home as a reminder of the love and happiness that brought us all together today. When the bottle is discovered, they will revisit their original letter, and share the correspondence of the person that found the bottle.

(Groom and Bride may roll up letter, tying it with twine or string and place it in bottle with cork.)

(Officiant): **Groom** and **Bride**, should you ever find your marriage enduring insurmountable hardships, you are, as a couple, to take a trip to the beach, any beach. You are to bring the copies of this letter with you, and when you get to the beach, you are to separate and each read the letter alone. After you have both read the letter and had time to reflect back on this day when you were married, you are to place one of the letters in another bottle and again throw it into the sea. This symbolizes that no matter the hardships in your life, because of the love you two have found and share together, your relationship will endure.

The hope is, however, that your original bottle will be found. The thoughts shared between you and the person who finds the bottle, hopefully, will inspire you to return to this very beach in celebration of the life that began with this bottle being tossed into the sea.

Groom and **Bride**, you may toss your Message in a Bottle into the sea.

(Groom and Bride throw bottle into sea.)

Note: Include your own love story in your letter along with a request for marital or life advice. Be sure to include your name and address in your letter so whoever finds it can respond.

You will need:
• a bottle with a cork
• pen and paper for your love letter
• string or twine to tie around letter
• sand to put in bottle *(optional)*

Native American Wedding Vase

(Native American)

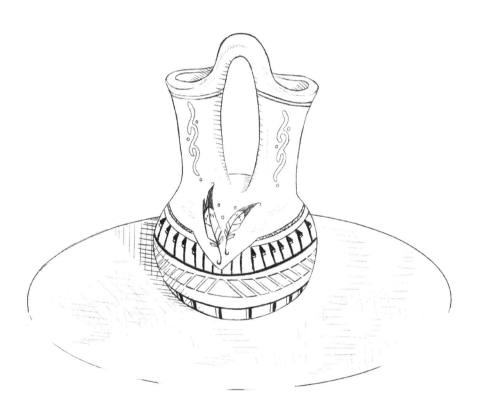

NATIVE AMERICAN WEDDING VASE *(Native American)*

The "Native American Wedding Vase" tradition originated with the Navajo, Pueblo, Hopi and Cherokee nations. To celebrate the wedding ceremony, the indigenous people used a uniquely designed handmade pottery jar, which, when translated, means wedding vase.

(Officiant): **Groom** and **Bride** have chosen to include a Native American tradition in their ceremony today. They both will drink from a Native American Wedding Vase to illustrate the joining of their hearts and lives into one common destiny. Let me explain the symbolism of the wedding vase.

(Officiant holds up wedding vase and points to each part as he explains symbolism.)

(Officiant): The Native American Wedding Vase features a graceful double neck with two symmetrical spouts coming out of the top where the handles are attached. The spouts, which symbolize the Bride's and Groom's individual lives, are joined by a rounded looped handle, which represents the bridge that joins their two lives together. The round space created between the neck and handle symbolizes the circle of life. The body of the vase is hand etched with artistic designs that reflect the various styles characteristic of each pueblo. Since clay has a history of symbolizing life and is a product of Mother Earth, Native Americans believe that each piece of pottery possesses a spirit.

Prior to the ceremony, a medicine man traditionally was responsible for preparing a love potion made of sweet nectar and holy water that would link the couple together for eternity. Today, however, the Groom's parents prepare the love potion, which usually is an herbal tea.

The Bride will take a sip from one spout. *(Bride sips.)* She will offer it to the Groom, who drinks from the opposite spout. *(Groom sips.)* Finally, they both will drink from the vase at the same time. It is said, if the couple can drink from the vase at the same time without spilling a single drop, then cooperation, compromise and great understanding always will be part of their marriage. Let's watch and see if that will be true!

(Couple drinks from each spout simultaneously. Officiant may make comment if liquid spills.)

(Officiant): The Native American Wedding Vase is a treasured heirloom and is protected always. It is never broken, discarded, destroyed or even sold as a work of art. If not kept by the Bride and Groom, it is usually passed down to the next generation for their wedding, or given as a wedding gift to another couple.

Groom and **Bride**, drinking from this vase together symbolizes the joining of your two lives into one. Even though you remain as individuals and drink from separate spouts, the love potion that links your hearts and destinies forever is shared from the same vessel—the Native American Wedding Vase.

I would like to bless your marriage with an old Native American (Apache/Cherokee/Navajo) wedding blessing *(based on selected wedding blessing)*.

Native American Blessings

Apache Wedding Blessing

Now you will feel no rain, for each of you will be a shelter for the other.
Now you will feel no cold, for each of you will be warmth to the other.
Now there will be no loneliness, for each of you will be a companion to the other.
Now you are two persons, but there is only one life before you.
Go now to your dwelling place, to enter the days of your togetherness.
May beauty surround you both in the journey ahead and through all the years.
May happiness be your companion, and may your days together be good and long upon the earth.
~Unknown

Cherokee Marriage Prayer

God in heaven above, please protect the ones we love.
We honor all you created as we pledge our hearts and lives together.
We honor Mother Earth and ask for our marriage to be abundant and grow stronger
    through the seasons.
We honor fire and ask that our union be warm and glowing with love in our hearts.
We honor wind and ask that we sail through life safe and calm as in our Father's arms.
We honor water to clean and soothe our marriage that it may never thirst for love.
All the forces of the universe you created.
We pray for harmony and true happiness as we forever grow young together. Amen. *~Unknown*

Navajo Wedding Blessing

Be swift like the wind in loving each other.
Be brave like the sea in loving each other.
Be gentle like the breeze in loving each other.
Be patient like the sun who waits and watches the four changes of the earth in loving each other.
Be shining like the morning dawn in loving each other.
Be proud like the tree that stands without bending in loving each other.
Be brilliant like the rainbow colors in loving each other.
Now, forever, forever, there will be no more loneliness
    because your worlds are joined together. Forever, forever. *~Unknown*

Note: Native American Wedding Vases may be found on these websites:
www.palmstrading.com/native-american-pottery/native-wedding-vases/
www.kachinahouse.com/native-american-pottery/wedding-vases

You will need:
• authentic Native American Wedding Vase
• water or tea to drink from vase
• table to set vase on

Oathing Stone

(Scottish/Celtic)

OATHING STONE *(Scottish/Celtic)*

The "Oathing Stone" ritual is an old Scottish/Celtic tradition where the Bride and Groom place their hands upon a stone while saying their wedding vows in order to "set their vows in stone."

(Officiant): The vows that **Groom** and **Bride** are about to make will provide a firm foundation for the life they will share together from this day forward. To symbolize this, they will be borrowing from an old Celtic tradition called the "Oathing Stone."

You have heard the phrase "set in stone?" It was believed that by holding a stone while declaring their wedding vows, the Bride and Groom "cast their vows in stone" forever. An oath that was given near a stone was considered more binding. This evolved into the Bride and Groom holding an engraved stone as they spoke their wedding vows, which is what we will witness today.

There is an old Celtic saying that goes like this: "I wrote our name in the sand and a wave washed it away. I wrote our name in the sky and the wind blew it away. I wrote our name in stone and forever there it will stay."

This particular Oathing Stone is engraved with the names of the Bride and Groom and the date of their wedding. It will serve as a precious keepsake of the vows they have made on their wedding day. They will place their hands upon the Oathing Stone as they give their promises to each other and pledge their "oath of love" forever.

(Bride and Groom hold stone together and say wedding vows.)

Note: The Oathing Stone may be engraved with the names of the Bride and Groom and their wedding date or a phrase or symbol that is special to them. It then becomes a precious keepsake and a reminder of their wedding vows that are the foundation of their marriage. The Oathing Stone may be used as a paper weight, placed in a terrarium or displayed in a shadow box.

Guest Participation with Wishing/Blessing Stones
(optional)

(Officiant to guests): When you arrived, you were given a stone to hold in your hand during the wedding ceremony. **Groom** and **Bride** chose these "Blessing Stones" as symbols of your special relationship, love, good wishes and heartfelt blessings to them. As you hold the Blessing Stone in your hand, please reflect for a moment on your wishes and blessings for this couple for love, happiness, prosperity and unity as they exchange their wedding vows. Following the ceremony, the Bride and Groom invite you to place the stones with your personal blessing for them into the container provided. These Blessing Stones will serve as a lasting reminder of your presence here and the love they shared with you on their wedding day.

You will need:
- a stone or river rock (engraved with names, initials, wedding date, image or phrase)
- Wishing/Blessing Stones for guests *(optional)*

Ribbons and Rings

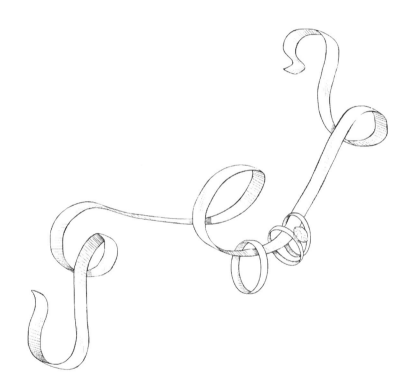

RIBBONS AND RINGS

This is a unique way of giving the rings when the Officiant says, "M
Instead of the Best Man, Maid of Honor or Ring Bearer handi
rings when asked, the Bride and Groom may choose to perforr
Rings," which allows the guests to participate.

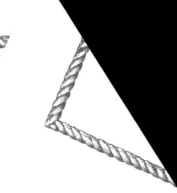

Ribbons and Rings Procedure

- *Best Man goes to back row aisle seat on Groom's side with a long, long piece of ribbon*
- *He guides ribbon as guests pass it forward to those in aisle seats in front of them, eventually to Groom, Officiant and Bride, then back down Bride's side to guests sitting in aisle seats until it reaches last person, making a giant U shape*
- *Best Man returns to end of aisle, where he strings one ring onto left side of ribbon and one ring onto right side of ribbon*
- *Guests holding ribbon will move rings forward toward Officiant and couple*

(Officiant explains symbolism): All of you, family and friends, who have gathered here today, have had a hand in shaping who the Bride and Groom are as individuals, and also who they are as a couple. So it is fitting that you, too, have a hand in offering your best wishes and blessings to the vows that unite **Groom** and **Bride** today. This will be demonstrated by a ceremony called "Ribbons and Rings."

(Officiant): The rings will be passed on a ribbon from the back to the front, ending up with the Officiant. Please offer a silent wish or blessing for the couple as you move the rings forward on the ribbon toward them.

(When rings get to Officiant, he uses a pair of scissors to cut ribbon and collect rings.)

(Officiant): These scissors represent a married couple. Sometimes the two sides will move in opposite directions, but, anyone who tries to come between them…will…be…punished! *(Snip!)*

Groom and **Bride**, these rings now hold all the blessings and good wishes of your family and friends who have passed them along to you through these ribbons of love that tie you all together.

(Bride and Groom then exchange rings and ring vows.)

You will need:
- wedding rings
- very long ribbon to hold rings (to go from back to front to back of venue again—in a U shape)
- scissors

Ring Warming

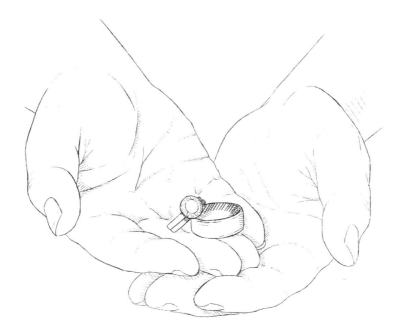

RING WARMING

The "Ring Warming" ritual is a wonderful way to involve family and friends in your wedding. The wedding rings are placed in a bag, bowl, pillow, or tied to ribbons, which may be passed around to all your guests, or to only a select group such as your family members. While holding the rings, each person is asked to make a wish or say a blessing for the newlyweds. When the rings return to the Bride and Groom, they exchange their rings with one another.

This ceremony symbolizes that good, successful marriages need support and love from their families and friends, and in return, the couple enhances the world around them.

The Ring Warming ritual is usually done right before the Ring Exchange unless a number of guests are asked to "warm the rings." Then it may be started earlier to ensure enough time for everyone to "warm the rings" by the time the Ring Exchange takes place.

Ring Warming Ceremony

(Officiant): During this ceremony **Groom** and **Bride** will exchange their wedding rings. These rings are the visible sign of their commitment to one another. However, recognizing how important your support of their marriage is, **Groom** and **Bride** have asked for you to participate in a "Ring Warming" ritual.

May I have the rings please? *(Officiant holds up rings and explains process.)*

(Officiant): We are going to pass the wedding rings around to all of you. We ask that you, their family and friends, take a brief moment while you hold their rings and say a blessing for their marriage, or make a wish for health and happiness and all that is good in life. Please warm their rings with your love and blessings, then pass them on to the next person who will do the same.

Two people in love do not live in isolation. Their love is a source of strength with which they may nourish not only each other but also the world around them. And in turn, we, their community of family and friends, have a responsibility to this couple. By our steadfast love, care and respect, we can support their marriage and the new family they are creating today.

(Rings are passed around to guests who make a wish or say a blessing for couple before passing them to next person.)

(Officiant): These rings that have come back to us not only contain precious metal, they contain that which is more precious, that which is priceless—your love and friendship and pledge of support for this union. Thank you, everyone, for loving **Groom** and **Bride** in this way.

You will need:
- wedding rings
- ribbons, bag, box, pillow or container to hold rings while passed (placing rings in something helps to avoid dropping or losing them, and tying with ribbons ensures they will stay together)
- music, which may be played while rings are passed

Rose Presentation

ROSE PRESENTATION

Rose Presentation~Version 1

(Present roses to mothers upon entrance and exit)

The "Presentation of the Rose" symbolizes the merging of the Bride's and Groom's families. When the Bride enters, she has in her possession two roses, usually red. As she approaches the altar, the Bride will stop and offer a rose and a kiss to her mother or significant mother figure. In doing this, she is expressing her gratitude for preparing her for this moment and for receiving the man she is about to marry into her family. When the ceremony has ended and she and the Groom exit, the Bride will stop and offer a rose and a kiss to the Groom's mother or significant mother figure. In doing this, she is expressing her gratitude for preparing her new husband for this moment and for receiving her into the Groom's family. A variation you may consider is to present roses to both mothers at the same time, either upon the entrance or upon the exit.

Rose Presentation~Version 2

(Present roses to each other as first gift, then to mothers)

(Officiant): **Groom** and **Bride** have chosen to give each other a rose, which is their first gift as husband and wife.

(Officiant will give both Bride and Groom a rose and they present their rose to each other.)

(Officiant): This rose was born of the tiniest of seeds and has blossomed into the beautiful flower it is today. And so it is with your relationship. It began as a small feeling that grew and eventually blossomed into something beautiful. And now you stand before us today to make a commitment to each other as husband and wife.

Since you know that love must be shared, it is your desire to share these first gifts with two very special people, two people who helped to prepare you for this moment and molded you into the individuals you are today.

(Bride and Groom present roses to mothers or significant mother figures and offer a hug or a kiss.)

Rose Presentation~Version 3

(Present roses to each other as first gift, and symbol of unspoken love)

(Officiant): **Groom** and **Bride**, today you will receive the most honorable titles that exist between a man and a woman—the titles of husband and wife. You have chosen to give each other a rose as your first gift. In the language of flowers, the rose is considered a symbol of love, and a single rose means only one thing—"I love you." So it is appropriate that your first gift to each other as husband and wife will be a single rose. Please exchange your gifts.

(Bride and Groom present each other with a rose.)

(Officiant): **Groom** and **Bride**, because you have given and received this symbol of love, I would encourage you to choose one very special place in your home for roses. Then on each anniversary, you both may take a rose to that special place as a recommitment to your marriage, and express with this symbol that your marriage is a marriage based on love.

In every marriage, there are times when it is difficult to verbalize certain feelings. Sometimes, we hurt those whom we love most, then find it difficult to say, "I am sorry," or "Please forgive me," or "I need you." When you simply cannot find these words, leave a rose at your specially chosen place, and let that rose say what matters most—"I still love you." The other should accept this rose for the words that cannot be found, and remember that the unspoken love is the hope you share and the faith you have in your future together as husband and wife.

Note: Red roses traditionally are used because red symbolizes love, but other colors may be used. However, red roses show up better in photos.

You will need: *(depending on version used)*
- roses for each mother *(Versions 1 and 2)*
- roses for Bride and Groom *(Versions 2 and 3)*
- vase for roses *(optional)*
- table to hold roses

Salt Ceremony

Covenant of Salt

(Christian/Indian)

SALT CEREMONY *(Covenant of Salt~Christian/Indian)*

Covenant of Salt History

(Officiant shares history): The "Covenant of Salt" is an ancient covenant mentioned in the Old Testament. It was a means of sealing an agreement between two parties. In fact, the Arabic word for "salt" and "treaty" is the same word. The expression, "There is salt between us" represents the cementing of a friendship.

The Covenant of Salt indicates a binding contract. In the Bible, when a contract was made, each party put a pinch of salt into the pocket of the other person. It was said that when each grain of salt could be sorted, identified, and returned to the rightful owner, then, and only then, could the contract be broken.

In Bible times, salt was a very important and valued commodity, and that is why it was used in ancient wedding ceremonies to seal the Bride's and Groom's wedding vows. There was a close connection between salt and promises.

Salt is essential to life; it adds flavor, heals and preserves. Similarly, your commitment to each other will add flavor to your marriage, will provide healing when you are hurting, and, more importantly, will preserve your relationship, as you will have "salt between you."

Covenant of Salt~*Version 1*

(Toss the salt)

(Officiant): **Groom** and **Bride** have chosen to include an ancient ritual in their wedding today, a ritual called the "Covenant of Salt." As one of the earth's purest substances, salt symbolizes purity. The Covenant of Salt is a promise, an expression of eternal love, faithful dedication and permanent commitment. In a marriage, the Covenant of Salt is a binding promise between God, a woman and a man.

The Bride and Groom will be given a small amount of salt in their hands. As they proclaim their love, dedication and commitment to each other and to God, they will cast their salt upward into the wind. As the salt is blown away and eventually lands, the covenant is established.

(Bride and Groom are given salt and toss the salt into the wind.)

(Officiant): **Groom** and **Bride**, there is only one way to break the covenant. Until you are able to pick up every grain of salt that was cast into the wind, you are not released from this marriage. Can you ever collect all the salt grains again? Of course not. Then God can never break the covenant you are making with him. And neither should either of you break the vows you have made with one another. And so are you bound by this Covenant of Salt, each to the other and both to the Lord for all the days of your lives.

Covenant of Salt ~ *Version 2*

(Taste the salt)

(Officiant): **Groom** and **Bride** desire to seal this commitment between one another and God, and so they are giving permission to hold each other accountable to the promises made here today. Because they want to preserve these promises, they will partake of the "Covenant of Salt."

(Bride and Groom take forefingers of their right hands, dip it into water from a bowl and put their finger in salt that is provided in separate container. They put salt in their spouse's mouth, usually on tongue as they open their mouths.)

(Just before salt is put in the mouth, the one receiving salt says his/her choice of one of the following vows.)
(Groom/Bride): In the name of my Lord Jesus Christ, I vow to do all that I promise for my wife/ husband, so help me God.

(Groom/Bride): **Bride/Groom**, in the company of our family and friends, with this gift of salt, I pledge to uphold the promises I have made to you this day.

Covenant of Salt ~ *Version 3*

(Blend the salt)

This Covenant of Salt ritual is similar to the Unity Sand ceremony. Three containers are needed: two salt shakers or small vials and one Unity Salt Bottle.

(Officiant): The Bride and Groom have chosen to include a special ritual in their wedding today— the "Covenant of Salt."

The Covenant of Salt is a promise, an expression of eternal love, faithful dedication and permanent commitment. In a marriage, the Covenant of Salt is a binding promise between God, a woman and a man.

These two vials of salt represent the individual lives of **Groom** and **Bride**. Salt is considered to be one of the earth's purest substances and, therefore, symbolizes purity. So when you combine your salt into the Unity Salt Bottle, not only are you joining your lives together as one, but you are making a commitment to keep your marriage pure before God and man.

(Bride and Groom combine their individual vials of salt into the Unity Salt Bottle.)

(Officiant): **Groom** and **Bride**, there is only one way to break the covenant. Until you are able to separate every grain of salt in this bottle, you are not released from this marriage. Can you ever collect all the salt grains again? Of course not. Then God can never break the covenant you are making with him. And neither should either of you break the vows you have made with one another. And so are you bound by this Covenant of Salt, each to the other and both to the Lord for all the days of your lives.

Note: Colored salt is not used because then, although it would be difficult, you would be able to separate your salt from your spouse's salt and it would no longer be an unbreakable agreement.

Covenant of Salt~Version 4

(Exchange salt from pouches)

(Officiant): The Bride and Groom will be making a special covenant today, which is illustrated by an ancient tradition called the "Covenant of Salt."

Groom and **Bride**, you have symbolized your commitment by the giving and receiving of rings. This covenant is a pledge between you both as you have committed to one another for the rest of your lives. This exchange of salt will embody the strength your marriage will hold. By combining your lives together, your union will be as difficult to separate as these grains of salt. The salt covenant made here today symbolizes the irreversible agreement your union represents. It shall never be divided or revoked, but will endure the challenges of life and withstand the tests of time.

(Groom and Bride exchange pinches of salt from their pouches by placing some of their own salt into the other's pouch.)

(Officiant): And so are you bound by this Covenant of Salt, each to the other for all the days of your lives.

Indian Salt Ceremony

(Exchange salt with family members)

Indian weddings often include a salt ceremony where the Bride passes a handful of salt to her Groom without spilling any. He then passes it back to her and the exchange is repeated three times. She then performs the salt exchange with the Groom's family members, which symbolizes blending her life with theirs.

(Officiant): The Bride and Groom will pass a handful of salt between them three times without spilling any of it, hopefully. The Bride then will exchange the salt with all the members of the Groom's family to symbolize blending in with her new family.

(Bride and Groom pass salt between them three times. Bride exchanges salt with Groom's family.)

(Officiant): Just as salt blends in and adds taste to any dish, may you, **Bride**, blend in with your new family and add flavor by contributing to its well-being. And most of all, may you season it with love always.

Note: Salt Ceremony usually takes place after the wedding vows and ring exchange.

You will need:
- white salt *(all versions)*
- container to hold salt *(Version 1, 2, and Indian Version)*
- bowl of water *(Version 1)*
- three glass vials *(Version 3)*
- two pouches *(Version 4)*

Sand Blending

(Hawaiian)

SAND BLENDING *(Hawaiian)*

Sand Blending~*Version 1*

(Couple only, with Minister/Officiant representing God)

Note: Use different colored sand for Bride and Groom. Neutral colored or white sand is used for foundation and top layer sand (God sand). Fine glitter may be mixed with "God sand."

(Officiant): **Groom** and **Bride**, today you are making a commitment to share the rest of your lives with each other. Your relationship is symbolized through the pouring together of these individual vessels of sand, which is called a "Sand Blending" ceremony.

1) Officiant pours a layer of sand in bottom of Unity Sand Vase
I will pour the first layer of sand into the Unity Sand Vase. It is always important to have a good, solid foundation to build upon. So the first layer of sand represents God, who is the foundation of your marriage. We then will build the rest of the layers on that foundation.

2) Groom pours his layer of sand, then Bride pours her layer of sand
Groom, through the sands of time you have grown into the person you are today. This vessel of sand represents all that you were, all that you are, and all that you will ever be. **Bride**, through the sands of time you have grown into the person you are today. This vessel of sand represents all that you were, all that you are, and all that you will ever be. As you each pour your separate vessel of sand, it signifies your lives prior to this moment—individual and unique.

3) Bride and Groom simultaneously pour their sands into Unity Sand Vase
Now as you blend the sands together, it illustrates your coming together in marriage and symbolizes the blending of your two hands, two hearts and two lives into one.

4) Officiant pours a final layer of sand on top of other layers
This final layer of sand again represents God, who not only is the foundation of your marriage, but also who seals your marriage with his blessing and covers you both with his love.

5) Final words by Officiant
Groom and **Bride**, just as these grains of sand can never be separated again, so may your lives be blended together for all eternity.

Note: You may substitute the first and last layer (layers 1 and 4) with Version 6 if you prefer non-religious text.

You will need:
- three vessels (Officiant, Groom, Bride)
- one Unity Sand Vase
- different colored sand for each participant (Officiant, Groom, Bride)
- glitter, which may be mixed in with "God sand" *(optional)*
- table for all items

Sand Blending~*Version 2*

(Includes children of Bride and Groom)

Note: Use different colored sand for each person. Neutral colored or white sand is used for foundation and top layer (God sand). Fine glitter may be mixed with "God sand."

(Officiant): **Groom** and **Bride**, today you are making a commitment to share the rest of your lives with each other. Your new family relationship is symbolized through the pouring together of these individual vessels of sand, which is called a "Sand Blending" ceremony.

1) Officiant pours a layer of sand in bottom of Unity Sand Vase
I will pour the first layer of sand into the Unity Sand Vase. It is always important to have a good, solid foundation to build upon. So the first layer of sand represents God, who is the foundation of your marriage and your family. We then will build the rest of the layers on that foundation.

2) Groom pours layer of sand, then Bride pours layer of sand
Your separate vessels of sand represent all that you were, all that you are, and all that you will ever be. You each will pour your own layer of sand, signifying your individual lives before today. It also is a reminder that even though you become one, you still retain your individuality and uniqueness that made you first fall in love with each other.

3) Children pour their individual layers of sand
Each child will pour their own layer of colored sand, which represents their individuality and provides their own unique color to make this rainbow complete. **Child/ren**, you may pour your sand now.

4) Bride and Groom simultaneously pour their sands into Unity Sand Vase
Groom and **Bride**, you will pour your individual vessels of sand together, symbolizing the joining of your two hands, two hearts and two lives into one.

5) Bride, Groom and children all pour their sands into Unity Sand Vase simultaneously
Now all of you will pour your sands together into the Unity Sand Vase at the same time, which symbolizes the blending of your lives and the blending of your families into one new family.

6) Officiant pours final layer of sand on top of other layers
This final layer of sand represents God, who not only is your foundation, but also who seals your marriage and new family with his blessing and covers you all with his love.

7) Final words by Officiant
Just as these grains of sand can never be separated again, so may your lives be blended together for all eternity.

You will need:
• vessels for Officiant, Groom, Bride, each child, plus Unity Sand Vase
• different colored sand for each participant (Officiant, Groom, Bride, children)
• glitter, which may be mixed in with "God sand" *(optional)*
• table for all items

Sand Blending~*Version 3*

(Includes parents and children of Bride and Groom)

Note: Use different colored sand for each person involved. Neutral colored sand is used for foundation. Fine glitter may be mixed with white sand used for top layer ("God sand").

(Officiant): **Groom** and **Bride**, today you are making a commitment to share the rest of your lives with each other. Your new family relationship is symbolized through the pouring together of these individual vessels of sand, which is called a "Sand Blending" ceremony.

1) Parents of Bride and Groom each pour a layer of sand in bottom of Unity Sand Vase
It is your parents who pour the first layer of sand, the foundation, into the Unity Sand Vase, because it is your parents who laid the foundation for your lives. Because of that foundation, you have grown into the individuals you are today, which has prepared you for this moment in time.

2) Groom pours layer of sand, then Bride pours layer of sand
Your separate vessels of sand represent all that you were, all that you are, and all that you will ever be. You each will pour your own layer of sand, signifying your individual lives before today. It also is a reminder that even though you become one, you still retain your individuality and uniqueness that made you first fall in love with each other.

3) Children pour their individual layers of sand
Each child will pour their own layer of colored sand, which represents their individuality and provides their own unique color to make this rainbow complete. **Child/ren**, you may pour your sand now.

4) Bride and Groom simultaneously pour their sands into Unity Sand Vase
Groom and **Bride**, you will pour your individual vessels of sand together, symbolizing the joining of your two hands, two hearts and two lives into one.

5) Bride, Groom and children all pour their sands into Unity Sand Vase simultaneously
Now all of you will pour your sands together into the Unity Sand Vase at the same time, which symbolizes the blending of your lives and the blending of your families into one new family.

6) Officiant pours final layer of sand on top of other layers
This final layer of sand represents God, who seals your marriage and new family with his blessing and who covers you all with his love.

7) Final words by Officiant
Just as these grains of sand can never be separated again, so may your lives be blended together for all eternity.

You will need:
- vessels for Officiant, Groom, Bride, each child, couple's parents, plus Unity Sand Vase
- different colored sand for each participant (Officiant, Groom, Bride, children, parents)
- glitter, which may be mixed in with "God sand" *(optional)*
- table for all items

Sand Blending~Version 4

(Christian variation includes parents and children of Bride and Groom; Minister/Officiant represents God)

Note: Parents use stones for foundation. Officiant uses neutral colored sand *(mixed with glitter optional)* to represent God as mortar. Bride, Groom and children each use different colors of sand for individuality.

(Officiant): **Groom** and **Bride**, today you are making a commitment to share the rest of your lives with each other. Your new family relationship is symbolized through the pouring together of these individual vessels of sand, which is called a "Sand Blending" ceremony.

1) Parents of Bride and Groom place stones in bottom of Unity Sand Vase
These stones represent the foundation of your marriage. It is your parents who place these stones in the Unity Sand Vase because they are the ones who laid the foundation for your lives. Because of that foundation, you have grown into the individuals you are today, which has prepared you for this moment in time.

2) Officiant pours layer of sand over stones, representing God, the mortar of marriage
This layer of sand represents God, who is the mortar that holds the foundation stones together.

3) Groom pours his individual layer of sand into Unity Sand Vase
This layer of sand represents you as an individual, **Groom**, all that you were, all that you are, and all that you will ever be.

4) Officiant pours layer of sand over Groom's layer
This layer of sand symbolizes God covering you, **Groom**, with his *Wisdom* so you will make good and wise choices for your family and provide for them with care.

5) Bride pours her individual layer of sand into Unity Sand Vase
This layer of sand represents you as an individual, **Bride**, all that you were, all that you are, and all that you will ever be.

6) Officiant pours layer of sand over Bride's layer
This layer of sand symbolizes God covering you, **Bride**, with his *Peace* so you will not worry about the children, or finances, or the house, or anything else that makes a woman worry.

7) Children pour their individual layers of sand
Each child will pour their own layer of colored sand, representing their individual and unique personalities, and providing their own distinct color to make this rainbow complete.

8) Officiant pours layer of sand over Children's layer
Child/ren, this layer of sand symbolizes God covering you with his *Joy* so you will bring laughter and happiness to your home and family. Then you can bring that same joy to your parents by listening to them, obeying them and always making them proud of who you are.

9) Bride and Groom pour sand together, symbolizing the joining of their lives in marriage
Groom and **Bride**, you will pour your individual vessels of sand together, symbolizing the joining of your two hands, two hearts and two lives into one.

10) Officiant pours layer of sand over Bride and Groom's layer
This layer of sand symbolizes God, covering you, **Groom** and **Bride**, with his *Faithfulness* so you will learn that he is faithful to his promises, and that you can trust him no matter what circumstances life may bring. When you learn to do that, then God, in turn, will give you the strength to trust each other and to be faithful to each other throughout your lives together.

11) Bride, Groom and children pour all vessels of sand together simultaneously into Unity Sand Vase
Now you all will pour your sand together at the same time into the Unity Sand Vase. This layer of sand symbolizes the blending of your hearts, your lives and your families into one new family.

12) Officiant pours final layer of sand on top of other layers
This final layer of sand, once again, represents God, who seals your marriage and your family with his *Blessing* and who covers you all with his *Love*.

13) Final words by Officiant
Just as these grains of sand can never be separated again, so may your lives be blended together for all eternity.

Note: Although longer and more detailed, this version tells your story, includes your whole family, honors God, and makes many colorful layers in your Unity Sand Vase to treasure always.

You will need:
• vessels for Officiant, Groom, Bride, each child, couple's parents, plus Unity Sand Vase
• different colored sand for each participant (Officiant, Groom, Bride, children, parents)
• glitter, which may be mixed in with "God sand" *(optional)*
• stones for foundation laid by couple's parents
• table for all items

Sand Blending~*Version 5*

(Couple only; center vessel or all vessels are heart shaped)

A Heartful of Love

Note: Heart-shaped vessels are used. Center vessel only or all three vessels may be heart shaped.

(Officiant): Today, **Groom** and **Bride** have chosen to symbolize their love for each other with a "Sand Blending" ceremony.

The "sands of time" should remind us of our journey through life and all the moments that have brought us to this very special moment today.

Note that the Bride and Groom have chosen a glass heart in which to blend their sands. This vessel is made from sand melding together in clarity and purpose to make a single heart. The Bride's and Groom's lives also have been melding together with the purpose of joining their hearts in the bonds of marriage.

1) Groom pours a layer of his sand into center glass heart
Groom, this glass vessel/heart of sand represents you and the heart full of love you give to your Bride today. Please pour your love into the center vessel/heart.

2) Bride pours a layer of her sand into center glass heart
And **Bride**, this glass vessel/heart of sand represents you and the heart full of love you give to your Groom today. Please pour your love into the center heart.

3) Bride and Groom pour sand from their individual vessels/hearts into center heart simultaneously to blend their sands together. Fill heart vessel completely with sand
Groom and **Bride**, you will blend the sands from your two individual vessels/hearts into this single glass heart. This symbolizes the blending together of your two hearts to form one beautiful heart—the sharing of one life and one love.

4) Final words by Officiant
May this glass heart full of sand always be a reminder that your two hearts now beat as one. And may it remind you to always keep your hearts full of love as they are on this, your wedding day.

You will need:
- heart-shaped unity vessel
- two heart-shaped vessels (or other vessels) for Groom and Bride
- different colored sand for Groom and Bride
- table for all items

168

Sand Blending~*Version 6*
(Secular variation using Love Sand instead of God Sand)

Note: This version may be used for those who prefer a non-religious "Sand Blending" ceremony. The theme of love is substituted for God, so the "God sand" becomes "Love sand."

(The text for only first and last layers will change. The rest of the layers will remain the same.)

(Officiant): **Groom** and **Bride**, today you are making a commitment to share the rest of your lives with each other. Your relationship is symbolized through the pouring together of these individual vessels of sand, which is called a "Sand Blending" ceremony.

First layer of sand—Foundation Sand
(Officiant): I will pour the first layer of sand into the vessel. It is important to have a good, solid foundation to build upon. So the first layer of sand represents *Love*, which is the foundation of your marriage (and family). We then will build the rest of the layers on that foundation.

(Text for middle layers will be the same as text for other sand ceremonies—based on which sand ceremony version you choose.)

Top layer of sand—Sealing Sand
(Officiant): This final layer of sand again represents *Love*, which not only symbolizes the foundation of your marriage (and family), but *Love* also covers you and seals your marriage (and family) forever. *Love* is the one thing that will keep you together for always. I now will seal your marriage (and family) with *Love*.

You will need:
- vessels for all participants (Officiant, Groom, Bride, each child, parents, plus Unity Sand Vase)
- different colored sand for each participant (Officiant, Groom, Bride, children, parents)
- table for all items
- any other items listed on the version you choose (i.e., stones for foundation)

Sand Blending~*Version 7*

(Variation using Heirloom Hourglass as vessel)

(Officiant): For centuries, the hourglass has been considered an enduring symbol of the passage of time. Time is measured in moments—ordinary moments, special moments, and those "once-in-a-lifetime" moments we all experience as we travel through life. Today, we are witness to one of those "once-in-a-lifetime" moments as **Groom** and **Bride** become husband and wife.

In some ways, tomorrow will seem no different than yesterday. But today, your wedding day, your lives will be blended together just as you will blend this sand into the hourglass, and you will never, ever be the same again.

1) Groom pours his layer of sand, then Bride pours her layer of sand
Groom, through the sands of time you have grown into the person you are today. This vessel of sand represents all that you were, all that you are, and all that you will ever be. **Bride**, through the sands of time you have grown into the person you are today. This vessel of sand represents all that you were, all that you are, and all that you will ever be. As you each pour your separate vessels of sand, it signifies your lives prior to this moment—individual and unique.

2) Bride and Groom combine their sands into Heirloom Hourglass
Now as you blend your sands together into the hourglass, it symbolizes this once-in-a-lifetime moment where you will blend your two hands, two hearts and two lives into one.

Every time you turn the hourglass, the sands become more blended, just as your lives will become more blended the longer you share them together.

This "Heirloom Hourglass" is a lifelong symbol of your marriage. Every time you look at it, may it take you back to the magic of this special day and all the other special moments you will experience from this day forward.

Groom and **Bride**, remember that time will pass quickly. The moments will become hours… the hours become days…the days will turn into years…and you will say, "Where did the time go?" Make every moment count, for you can never get it back again. Cherish the time you have been given with each other. Every night before you go to sleep, turn the hourglass over, watch the sand flow through, and let it remind you that you have been blessed with yet another day of life with the one you love.

Just as these grains of sand can never be separated again, so may your lives be blended together forever and for all time.

Note: Heirloom Hourglass may be found at **www.heirloomhourglass.com**.

You will need:
• hourglass to hold sand
• different colored sand for Groom and Bride
• table for all items

Seven Steps

Seven Blessings

(Indian Hindu/Native American)

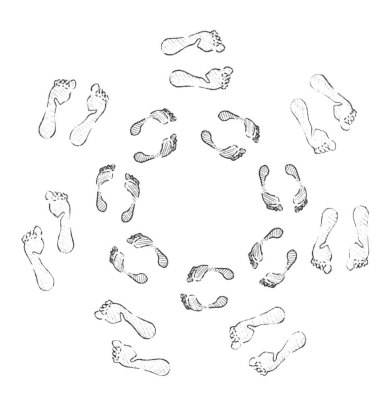

SEVEN STEPS *(Seven Blessings~Indian Hindu/Native American)*

Seven Steps~Indian Hindu *(Saptapadi)*

(Officiant): In the Hindu version of the "Seven Steps," known as "Saptapadi," the Bride's sari (dress) is tied in a knot to the Groom's kurta (shawl). The Bride's and Groom's pinky fingers are linked as he leads her in the Seven Steps, usually around a fire, or a lighted candle on a table. By walking around the fire together, they agree to these vows and accept the blessings given. These final steps are considered the most important part of the ceremony, sealing their bond forever.

(As couple takes steps around fire, they read vows and Officiant blesses them.)

Seven Steps Procedure

First step
(Couple): Let us take the first step to provide for our home and family. *(Couple takes step.)*
(Officiant): May this couple be blessed with an abundance of resources and comforts and be helpful to one another in all ways.

Second step
(Couple): Let us take the second step to develop physical, mental and spiritual powers. *(Couple takes step.)*
(Officiant): May this couple be strong and complement one another.

Third step
(Couple): Let us take the third step to increase our wealth by righteous means and proper use. *(Couple takes step.)*
(Officiant): May this couple be blessed with prosperity and riches on all levels.

Fourth step
(Couple): Let us take the fourth step to acquire happiness, knowledge and harmony by mutual love and trust. *(Couple takes step.)*
(Officiant): May this couple be eternally happy and content.

Fifth step
(Couple): Let us take the fifth step so we are blessed with healthy, virtuous and brave children. *(Couple takes step.)*
(Officiant): May this couple be blessed with a happy family life.

Sixth step
(Couple): Let us take the sixth step for self-restraint and longevity. *(Couple takes step.)*
(Officiant): May this couple live in perfect harmony in accordance with their personal values and their mutual promises.

Seventh step
(Couple): Finally, let us take the seventh step to be true companions and remain lifelong partners by this bond of marriage. *(Couple takes step.)*
(Officiant): May this couple always be the best of friends for all eternity.

Seven Steps~Native American

The origins of the "Rite of Seven Steps" are traced to many tribes in different parts of the continent and is not attributed to any one nation.

(Family and friends may join in a circle around Bride and Groom and hold hands as couple takes Seven Steps clockwise around fire.)

(Officiant): The Bride and Groom have chosen to include a Native American ritual in their ceremony today. The "Rite of the Seven Steps" ritual takes place around the sacred fire (or a candle on a table). The Groom takes the first step, then the Bride takes a step to join him. The Groom recites a vow to the Bride and, in return, the Bride gives her vow to the Groom. They will continue this procedure and take seven steps, each time reciting a new vow, until one encirclement of the fire is completed.

(As couple takes Seven Steps around fire, they read vows to each other.)

Seven Steps Procedure

Step 1~Groom
(Groom): O my beloved, our love has become firm by your walking the first step with me. Together we will share the responsibilities of the home, and provide food and clothes for our family. May the Creator bless us with noble children to share.

Step 1~Bride
(Bride): This is my commitment to you, my husband. Together we will share the responsibility of the home, food and children. I promise that I shall discharge all my share of the responsibilities for the welfare of the family and the children.

Step 2~Groom
(Groom): O my beloved, now you have walked with me the second step. May the Creator bless you. I will love you and you alone as my wife. I will fill your heart with strength and courage. This is my commitment and my pledge to you. May God protect our home and children.

Step 2~Bride
(Bride): My husband, at all times I shall fill your heart with courage and strength. In your happiness I shall rejoice. May God bless you and our honorable home.

Step 3~Groom
(Groom): O my beloved, now since you have walked three steps with me, our wealth and prosperity will grow. May God bless us. May we educate our children and may they live long and happy lives.

Step 3~Bride
(Bride): My beloved, I love you with single-minded devotion as my husband. I will treat all other men as my brothers. My devotion to you is pure and you are my joy. This is my commitment and my pledge to you.

Step 4~Groom

(Groom): O my beloved, it is a great blessing that you have now walked four steps with me. May the Creator bless you. You have brought favor and sacredness in my life.

Step 4~Bride

(Bride): O my husband, in all acts of righteousness, in material prosperity, in every form of enjoyment, and in those divine acts such as sacrifice, worship and charity, I promise you that I shall participate and always be with you.

Step 5~Groom

(Groom): O my beloved, now you have walked five steps with me. May the Creator make us prosperous; may the Creator bless us.

Step 5~Bride

(Bride): O my husband, I will share both in your joys and your sorrows. Your love will make me very happy.

Step 6~Groom

(Groom): O my beloved, by walking six steps with me, you have filled my heart with happiness. May I fill your heart with great joy and peace, time and time again. May the Creator bless you.

Step 6~Bride

(Bride): My husband, the Creator blesses you. May I fill your heart with great joy and peace. I promise that I will always be with you.

Step 7~Groom

(Groom): O my beloved, as you have walked the seven steps with me, our love and friendship have become inseparable and firm. We have experienced spiritual union in God. Now you have become completely mine. I offer my total self to you. May our marriage last forever.

Step 7~Bride

(Bride): My husband, by the law of the Creator and the spirits of our honorable ancestors, I have become your wife. Whatever promises I gave you, I have spoken them with a pure heart. All the spirits are witnesses to this fact. I shall never deceive you, nor will I ever intentionally let you down. I shall love you forever.

Note: A variation of this ceremony includes the couple exchanging gifts after every step to symbolize each vow given for their new life together. Typical gifts are corn~fertility; feathers~loyalty; stones~strength; wheat~provision; pine branch~longevity; shells~good fortune; and flowers~beauty and happiness.

You will need:
- note cards with blessings written on them for couple to carry as they walk in a circle
- gift items (if you choose to give gifts with each step—see gift suggestions in Note, above)
- handout explaining symbolism of gifts, if gifts are given

Shell Ceremony

SHELL CEREMONY

The "Shell Ceremony" is similar to the "Blessing/Wishing Stones Ceremony," except shells are used in place of stones. This is perfect for couples whose wedding ceremonies take place on or near the water or who just prefer shells instead of stones.

In Version 1, the shells are kept as keepsakes by the Bride and Groom. But in Version 2, at the end of the ceremony, the Bride, Groom and guests are directed to the water's edge to toss their Blessing Shells into the water together. Not only is it a special photographic moment, but is yet another way for everyone in attendance to be included in this special day.

An optional touch: Permanent markers may be provided for the guests to write their best wishes and blessings on the seashells—wishes such as Love, Joy, Peace, God's Blessings, Happiness, Health, Trust, Contentment, Laughter, whatever they wish for the couple. This way, the Bride and Groom can tangibly see the wish or blessing they have received.

Shell Ceremony~*Version 1*
(Shells kept in keepsake vessel)

Each guest is given a shell to hold during the ceremony and asked to make a wish or say a blessing for the Bride and Groom. The shells are collected and given to the couple to place in a keepsake vessel.

(Officiant): As you arrived, each of you were given a seashell. While you hold this shell in your hand, please take a moment and make a wish or say a blessing for this couple and their marriage —blessings such as Love, Joy, Peace, Happiness, Health, Patience, Wisdom, Prosperity, Laughter or Companionship.

(Pause for a moment as guests offer their blessing or make a wish.)

(Officiant): As you leave today, please put your seashells in the bowl provided. The Bride and Groom will place them in a keepsake vessel, along with some sand and pebbles, to be displayed in their home as a reminder of all the blessings and good wishes from you, their family and friends.

(Or, if a marker is used to write on the shells, Officiant may say the following.)

(Officiant): As you arrived, each of you were given a seashell. Please write a blessing or wish on the shell for this couple and their marriage. Single words may be used such as Love, Joy, Peace, Happiness, Health, Patience, Wisdom, Prosperity, Laughter or Companionship.

(Pause for a moment as guests write their blessing or wish on the shells.)

(Officiant): As you leave today, you may take your shells and place them in the bowl provided in order for the Bride and Groom to read and reflect upon them at a later time. They want to thank you for all the good wishes and blessings you have given to them on their wedding day.

Shell Ceremony~*Version 2*
(Shells tossed in water)

(Officiant): **Groom** and **Bride** are deeply grateful for each and every one of you here today. You all hold a place in their hearts, reserved for those they have chosen to call "family" and "friend." And because of this, they would like to ask you to participate in the blessing of their union with a "Shell Ceremony."

As you arrived, each of you were given a seashell to hold as you add your best wishes and blessings to the commitment made here today between the Bride and Groom.

Groom and **Bride**, when a commitment this strong is made by two people, the force of that commitment, of that love, of that courage, reaches out and touches all of us around you so our lives are changed as well, and we all share in a part of your love.

Like a seashell dropped in the ocean, the ripple of the love from this celebration extends and changes the world we live in.

I will ask you to take the shell you have been given and pause for a moment to make a wish or say a blessing for this couple and for their future together as husband and wife.

(Pause for a moment as guests offer their blessing or make a wish.)

(Officiant): In a moment we will toss our shells into the water. As the ripples cross and recross one another's, may our love and blessings also touch and retouch each other's lives. And should these shells wash up on the shore, may the blessings they contain reach out and touch those who find them so their lives are changed also. Then we all truly will share in a part of the love that has been expressed here today.

On the count of three, we will throw our shells into the sea. 1...2...3!

(Every one tosses shells into the water.)

Note: Officiant's words also may be spoken before accompanying couple to water's edge (during the ceremony). In this scenario, the only words spoken would be "On the count of three, we will throw our shells into the sea. 1...2...3!"

You will need:
- small smooth shells
- bowl to hold shells for guests to take
- markers to write wish or blessing on shells *(optional)*
- sand and pebbles to mix with shells *(optional)*
- keepsake container to display shells in home

Spice Blending

Spice of Life

SPICE BLENDING *(Spice of Life)*

(Officiant): Making a commitment to each other through marriage means you combine your gifts and talents, and together, you make a greater difference in the world than you would as individuals. Just as spices complete a recipe, you complete each other. You have chosen some spices (and herbs) to layer in this glass vessel one at a time, signifying your own personalities, your gifts and talents, along with your hopes and dreams for this marriage. In this way, you symbolically combine who you are. Just as the spices become intermingled and never will be the same again, so do your lives as you join in marriage.

In this "Spice Blending" ceremony, you will begin and end by pouring in salt, for salt is pure and essential to life. You may pour the first layer of salt.

(Couple pours first layer of salt together.)

(Officiant): This salt symbolizes pure love—God's love for you and your love for each other. This love will be the foundation upon which you build your life together. In the Bible, covenants of salt were made to ensure lasting and permanent pacts, as salt symbolized the eternal nature of the covenant. Your marriage also is such a covenant—endless, enduring and everlasting.

As you pour the following spices (and herbs), which you will layer between the salt, I will name each one and explain its symbolism.

Spice Blending Ceremony Sample

(Couple begins to pour one spice/herb at a time while Officiant reads meaning of each one.)

- Sage—wisdom and long life
- Rosemary—remembrance, love and fidelity
- Paprika—passion
- Poppy Seeds—prosperity
- Lavender—calm in the face of difficulties and seeing the opportunities in life
- Thyme—courage and strength

(Officiant): You may finish pouring the final layer of salt.

(Couple pours final layer of salt together.)

(Officiant): What a beautiful work of art you have created and a keepsake of this special day. Let this jar of spices symbolize how you have combined the essences of who you are and what you hope for into a blessed union of love. **Groom** and **Bride**, as you blend your love with the one who completes you, may you always find the "Spice of Life."

Symbolism of Spices and Herbs

- Allspice—acceptance of differences and endurance of hardships

- Anise and Star Anise—sweet dreams

- Basil—happiness, growing of love, fertility, good wishes

- Bay Leaf—good luck, ability to keep evil at bay, victory over everyday issues, calmness

- Caraway—ancient wisdom, remembrance

- Cardamom—sweet breath and fresh conversation

- Celery—ability to withstand hardship and loss

- Chives—happiness, ability to lighten the mood, old-time fun

- Cilantro—intensity, compliments, passion, hidden worth

- Cinnamon—stability, soft warmth

- Cloves—dignity, ability to withstand pain

- Coriander—magic, health, worthiness

- Cumin—engagement, listening, togetherness

- Dill—safety, security, courage, good spirits

- Fennel—strength, force, vision

- Garlic—strength, intensity, strong flavor

- Ginger—civility, traditions, old-fashioned niceness and hospitality

- Mace—action, stimulation, ability to stand together

- Marjoram—happiness

- Mustard—ability to get things out, ease in dealing with unpleasant things

- Nutmeg—sensuality, stimulation

- Onion—happiness, ability to lighten the mood, old-time fun

- Oregano—joy, appreciation of what you have

- Paprika—passion, spice, heat, warmth, vitality

- Parsley—festivity, hospitality, friendship, lightening of the load, silliness

- Hot Peppers—heat, warmth, spice, vitality, passion

- Black, Green, White Pepper—wealth, adventure, exploration

- Poppy Seeds—prosperity

- Rosemary—memory, health, wedding blessings, moderation

- Sage—wisdom, long life, calm energy

- Salt—protection, preservation, prevention of spoilage, healing, flavor

- Savory—balance

- Sesame—magic, openness, peace, calm

- Sugar—sweetness, caring

- Tarragon—support, inspiration, encouragement, unselfishness, flavor enhancer

- Thyme—courage, sacrifice, thriftiness, energy, powerful

- Turmeric—adaptive, ability to reduce problems, making the most of what you have

More Spice/Herb meaning links:
www.curreedy.com/missy/welcome-to-our-home/romance/herb-meaning/
www.weddingspicefavors.com/about/spice-symbolism-meaning/

Note: Couples who engage in the culinary arts often use the "Spice of Life" ritual to express their unity in marriage.

You will need:
- salt
- spices/herbs
- easy to pour containers to hold each spice/herb
- container to display combined spices/herbs
- spoon or scoop if not pouring spices/herbs *(optional)*

Tasting of the Elements

Sour~Bitter~Hot~Sweet

(African)

TASTING OF THE ELEMENTS *(Sour~Bitter~Hot~Sweet~African)*

The "Tasting of the Elements," an African tradition, demonstrates the promise to love your partner "for better, for worse, for richer, for poorer, in sickness and in health, till death do us part." Lemon, vinegar, cayenne pepper and honey are traditional choices used to represent the sour, bitter, hot and sweet parts of life. By tasting these elements, the couple demonstrates their symbolic commitment to share the seasons of life together, regardless of what life holds.

(Officiant): **Groom** and **Bride**, we don't know what the future holds, but we do know you are standing hand in hand, ready to face together whatever life may bring your way. You will demonstrate this commitment to share all the seasons of life with a ritual called the "Tasting of the Elements." Four elements are used—lemon, vinegar, cayenne pepper (or hot sauce) and honey. These represent the sour, bitter, hot and sweet parts of life.

Lemon~*Sour*

(Officiant): Please taste the first element—**Lemon**. *(Couple tastes lemon.)*
We can tell by the look on your faces that the lemon is very sour. There will be moments in your life and marriage when things also go sour—times of unhappiness and discontentment, conflict and frustration, times when you just want to make a face at the world and everyone in it, much like the faces you made when you tasted the lemon. It is then that you must show each other patience and understanding, working together to resolve the issues and to endure these sour moments, knowing that they, too, shall pass.

Vinegar~*Bitter*

(Officiant): Please taste the second element—**Vinegar**. *(Couple tastes vinegar.)*
Vinegar is a very bitter element and represents the bitter disappointments in life that inevitably will come at times. Disillusionment and discouragement can become a bitter taste in your mouth, and defeat, a bitter pill to swallow. You even may feel that life is not treating you fairly, causing bitter tears to be shed over the rejection you have experienced. The key, however, is to not let these things creep in and allow bitterness to take hold of your heart. To prevent that, you must give one another encouragement, hope, compassion, and, above all, tenderness, because tenderness will soften the heart and stave off potential bitterness.

Cayenne Pepper/Hot Sauce~*Hot*

(Officiant): Please taste the third element—**Cayenne Pepper**. *(Couple tastes pepper or hot sauce.)*
Hot, hot, hot! Because cayenne pepper is hot, it represents passion—a passion for love and a passion for life.

But sometimes passion comes in the form of anger, where hot tempers lead to heated arguments. Don't let your passion be wasted on anger. Instead, turn it into something that will kindle your love, not quench it.

(Officiant): Every marriage needs to fuel the fires of romance and add spice to the recipe of love. Take time to rekindle the passion and renew the spark that once burned in your hearts when you first fell in love.

Having a passion for life also gives us purpose. Purpose is the reason we journey. Passion is the fire that lights our way. Each of us has a fire in our heart for something. It is our goal in life to find it and keep it lit. So find your passion in life and you will find your purpose in life. Together, you will ignite the fires of passion in each other for love and for life.

Honey~*Sweet*

(Officiant): Please taste the fourth element—**Honey**. *(Couple tastes honey.)*
We saved the best for last. Of all the elements you tasted, this one brought a smile to your faces. A taste of honey—sweet! The honey represents the sweetness of married life and all it has to offer. Now you have a partner, a lover and a best friend with whom to share all of life's experiences in sweet communion. The honey also is a reminder that your marriage is blessed with the sweetness of your love for one another. There will be many sweet moments as you walk down the path of life together, moments with just the two of you and moments that also include your family and friends, creating many sweet memories along the way. Life is sweet…Love is sweeter…sweeter than honey!

Groom and **Bride**, remember that life is 10% what happens to you and 90% how you respond to it. So whether your experiences in life are sour, bitter, hot or sweet, always keep the promise to love your partner with this commitment: "for better, for worse, for richer, for poorer, in sickness and in health, till death do us part."

Note: You may use small glasses or bowls to hold the elements. If all elements are in liquid form (i.e., hot sauce may be substituted for cayenne pepper), you may take a small sip from each one. If they are in bowls, you may use either a spoon or your fingers to dip into the bowls for tasting each element. If fingers are used, do not use the same finger for each element, or by the time you get to the honey, it will taste bad, too. You also may choose to taste the honey yourself or to offer the honey to your partner instead.

The tasting of the elements can be a very humorous ritual due to the expressions on the Bride's and Groom's faces as they taste each element (which makes for great photos).

You will need:
- four containers to hold elements (small bowls, jars, glasses)
- spoons *(optional)*
- napkins or wet wipes (to wipe fingers, if fingers are used)
- lemon wedges or lemon juice
- vinegar
- cayenne pepper or hot sauce
- honey

Tea Ceremony

(Japanese/Chinese)

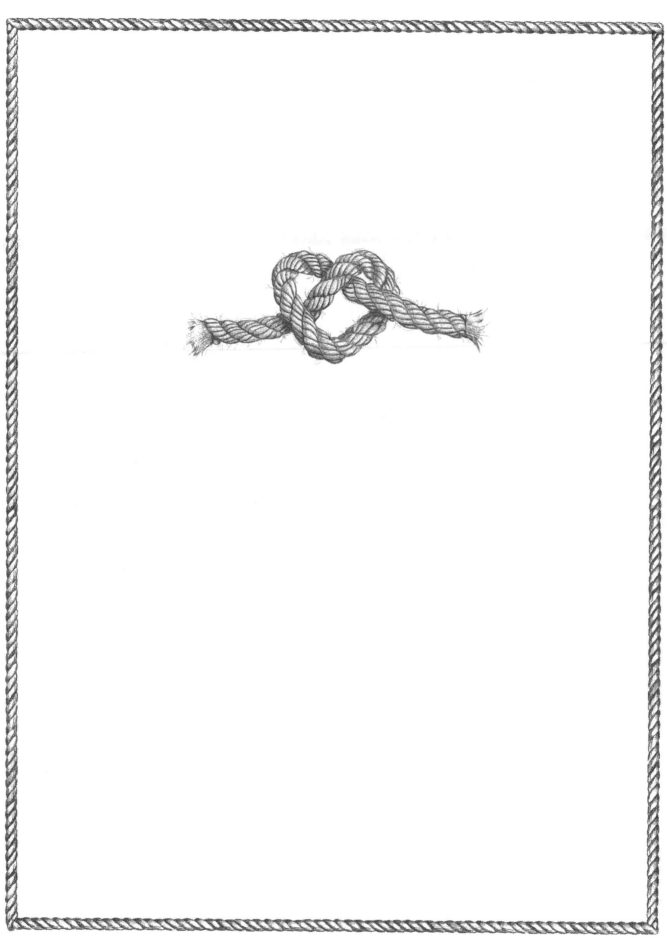

TEA CEREMONY *(Japanese/Chinese)*

Japanese Tea Ceremony ~ *(San San Ku Do)*

(Officiant): Groom and Bride have chosen to participate in the "San San Ku Do" or "Japanese Tea Ceremony." "San San Ku Do" means "three sets of three sips equals nine." Groom and Bride each take three sips of three cups, exchanging the cups with one another. This symbolizes a deepening and strengthening of the bonds between the couple. The small cup represents "heaven," the medium cup represents "earth," and the large cup represents "humanity." Three is a lucky number and can not be divided by two, which symbolizes two people who can not be divided. Nine is the biggest single number that can not be divided by two, which brings all the lucky elements to this wedding ceremony.

Japanese Tea Ceremony Procedure

- *Groom and Bride go to tea or sake station (small table) where three cups are stacked on top of each other, largest to smallest, along with a teapot filled with tea or sake*

- *Assistant fills smallest cup at top. A small amount of tea or sake is poured into cup three times. The first two times, tea/sake is not actually poured, but third time, cup is filled*

- *Same is true for drinking. Only third time does couple actually drink tea/sake*

- *Groom drinks from smallest cup with three sips. Groom passes cup to Bride and she drinks with three sips*

- *Assistant fills medium cup*

- *Bride drinks from medium cup with three sips. Bride passes cup to Groom and he drinks with three sips*

- *Assistant fills large cup*

- *Groom drinks from large cup with three sips. Groom passes cup to Bride and she drinks with three sips*

- *Groom and Bride return to altar and ceremony continues*

(An alternative is to have the Groom and Bride drink only three sips from one cup and each set of parents drink three sips from the other two cups, for a total of nine sips. This symbolizes the bond being created between the families that day.)

You will need:
- small table or tray to hold tea set
- teapot filled with tea or sake
- three cups (small, medium, large)
- designated assistant to pour tea
- Japanese music played in background *(optional)*

Chinese Tea Ceremony~(Jìng Chá)

In Chinese culture, the "Wedding Tea Ceremony," or "Jìng Chá," is a way for the Bride and Groom to pay respect to their families, and to formally acknowledge their families joining together. Traditionally, the tea ceremony is performed in private with the Bride and Groom kneeling in front of their parents, grandparents, aunts, uncles and other elders. As tea is served to each family member, the Bride and Groom thank them for their love and care. When each relative drinks the tea, they show their acceptance of the new member into their family. In return, the Bride and Groom receive "lai see" (red envelope), which contains money or jewelry. Sometimes, the jewelry is placed on the Bride and Groom by the giver of the gift at that moment.

In older traditions, the Bride served tea to her parents before the wedding as a symbolic gesture; her parents were essentially "giving her away." Later, after the ceremony, when the Groom brought his new Bride to his family's house, the tea ceremony was performed again with the Groom's parents welcoming the Bride into their family.

Today, many couples choose to include the tea ceremony either at the reception or during the actual wedding ceremony, serving both families of the couple at the same time. There are differing opinions, however, on the order of service, the position of the Bride and Groom, and whether it should be performed privately or publicly. Check with your "elders" for their guidance.

Chinese Tea Ceremony Procedure

(Officiant): The Bride and Groom have chosen to include a tea ceremony to show respect, to honor their families, and to formally introduce their beloved to each other's family.

(Officiant will call each family member to come forward to be served tea. Family members may sit in chairs provided.)

(Groom kneels on left cushion, while Bride kneels on cushion to his right, though some say reverse. Female relatives sit facing Groom; male relatives sit facing Bride. Designated "lucky lady" stands to side, along with assistant, ready to serve with tray of tea.)

(Groom serves male relative first, then female, asking each to drink the tea. Bride follows same pattern. They address each relative with proper title, e.g., "Grandmother Lihua, please drink tea." After relative drinks, they offer a verbal blessing and present couple with red envelopes of money or gold jewelry.)

Tea Ceremony Order of Service

- parents (first or second)
- grandparents (first or second)
- grand uncles and aunties *(optional)*
- uncles and aunties *(optional)*
- elder siblings *(optional)*
- elder cousins *(optional)*
- younger siblings *(optional)*
- nephews and nieces *(optional)*
- each other *(optional)*

Tea Ceremony Order of Service Sample

- *Groom serves tea to Father—Groom serves tea to Mother*
- *Bride serves tea to Father-in-law—Bride serves tea to Mother-in-law*
- *Groom's Father and Mother present couple with red envelopes of money or gold jewelry*
- *Groom serves tea to Father-in-law—Groom serves tea to Mother-in-law*
- *Bride serves tea to Father—Bride serves tea to Mother*
- *Bride's Father and Mother present couple with red envelopes of money or gold jewelry*
- *Groom serves tea to Grandfather—Groom serves tea to Grandmother*
- *Bride serves tea to Grandfather-in-law—Bride serves tea to Grandmother-in-law*
- *Groom's Grandfather and Grandmother present couple with red envelopes of money or gold jewelry*
- *Groom serves tea to Grandfather-in-law—Groom serves tea to Grandmother-in-law*
- *Bride serves tea to Grandfather—Bride serves tea to Grandmother*
- *Bride's Grandfather and Grandmother present couple with red envelopes of money or gold jewelry*
- *Groom serves tea to his Uncle—Groom serves tea to his Auntie*
- *Bride serves tea to Groom's Uncle—Bride serves tea to Groom's Auntie*
- *Groom's Uncle and Auntie present couple with red envelopes of money or gold jewelry*
- *Groom serves tea to Bride's Uncle—Groom serves tea to Bride's Auntie*
- *Bride serves tea to her Uncle—Bride serves tea to her Auntie*
- *Bride's Uncle and Auntie present couple with red envelopes of money or gold jewelry*
    And so on…

Note: There are many variations of the tea ceremony. Some start with the Groom's family while others begin with the Bride's family. Usually, you will serve paternal relatives (father's family) before maternal ones (mother's family), and offer tea to the man before the woman. Be sure to serve relatives in order of seniority for this shows respect. Bride and Groom may kneel for all relatives or for parents and grandparents only, while simply bowing to other relatives as they serve them tea.

The keepsake jewelry gifts are usually not worn (except on special occasions) but kept in a safe place and meant to be used only if the couple falls into financial difficulty. If the couple has no need to ever sell it, then the jewelry is to be passed down to their children for their own weddings.

You will need:
- teapot and four cups on tray (one or two tea sets may be used—if two, Bride's wedding set for Groom's side and Bride's mother's wedding set for Bride's side)
- tea (sweet tea to symbolize happiness and sweetness of marriage and new family relationships)
- red dates, lotus seeds in tea cups for luck and fertility *(optional)*
- two chairs (for elders to sit on)
- two red cushions (for Bride and Groom to kneel on)
- "lucky lady" (who blesses and serves tea) and an assistant (to clean cups between sips)
- narrator to read blessings if relatives do not wish to speak publicly *(optional)*
- Chinese music played in background *(optional)*

Tree Planting

Marriage Tree

TREE PLANTING *(Marriage Tree)*

Planting the "Marriage Tree" is a physical manifestation that symbolizes the growth of a marriage relationship. Together the Bride and Groom can see the tree grow just as their love grows, nurturing it every day in order to keep both the tree and their marriage alive.

The Bride and Groom gather two pots of soil, possibly from a special significant place, and plant a tree in the combined soil. They water it together with two watering cans or one shared watering can (perhaps with water from a meaningful place). You may consider including your guests or immediate family and friends. Ask them to add their own scatters of soil or seeds.

(Officiant): **Groom and Bride** will take part in the planting of the "Marriage Tree." The Marriage Tree symbolizes the roots of your relationship and the continued growth of your love as you walk down the path of life together. Each day you will watch the tree grow just as your love and marriage grows. But in order to keep both the tree and your marriage alive, they must be nurtured daily with your tender love and constant care.

Groom and Bride, may your relationship and your love for each other be like this tree you plant today. May it grow tall and strong. May it stand tall during the harsh winds and rains and storms, and may it come through unscathed. Like a tree, your marriage must be resilient. It must weather the challenges of life and the passage of time.

Like the tree you are planting today, marriage requires constant nurturing and nourishment. Just as you provide the sun, soil and water for this tree, you must provide the encouragement, trust and love needed on a daily basis to consciously nurture and nourish your connection to each other. Look at the tree every day to inspire you to grow and reach your fullest potential— just like this tree. *(Insert family participation words here.)*

Groom and **Bride**, remember that love is the root of all and everything we do. Love enriches our experiences and fills our lives with meaning. It gives us a firm base from which to grow, to learn, to change. It allows us to branch out and share our love freely with others. You may plant the Marriage Tree now.

(Groom and Bride add dirt from each of their pots to tree, then take turns watering sapling.)

Family Participation

If family members (such as parents) are participating in the ceremony, the Officiant will explain the significance with the following words.

(Officiant): Since it was **Groom's** and **Bride's** parents who gave them their roots and provided a base for their life together, then it is their parents (or mothers) who will add the base soil around the Marriage Tree. (Optional: To symbolize the blending of the Bride's and Groom's lives, as well as the joining of their two families, the soil they are adding to the tree comes from each family's land/garden.)

(Parents/Mothers come forward and add soil to pot first before Bride and Groom add their soil.)

(Officiant): I would like to close this Marriage Tree Ceremony with a blessing from the Bible. **Groom** and **Bride**, may your marriage be "…like a tree planted beside streams of water that bears its fruit in time and whose leaf never withers, but blossoms and flourishes in every season of your lives" *(Psalms 1:3 HCSB).* Amen.

(Tree may be transplanted to the desired place, i.e., their home, to symbolize the putting down of roots, longevity and strength of the marriage.)

Tree Reading 1 *(optional)*

(Officiant): One of the reasons to use a tree as a metaphor at a wedding ceremony is the incredible symmetry of trees. The root system of a healthy tree is as large and beautiful as the canopy. As you stand beneath the leafy spread, you stand on ground that is held together by an expansive root system that enriches and supports the earth. There is nothing a marriage needs more than the same sort of grounding a tree has. We must plant the tree, and our marriages, in soil that will nourish and support it. Carefully cultivated and protected, those roots will flourish and provide nutrients for the tree to grow to its fullest potential.

The foundation of your marriage must be firm. When you dig deeply into your lives, what are the strengths of your marriage that will support it always? How will you make sure there is enough space for the roots of your marriage to spread? Have you cleared out enough time in your life to accommodate your marriage? Your answers will determine how firm a foundation upon which your marriage rests.

The trunk of the tree can be relied on to support us. With good roots, we stand firm in one another's love. We can lean on one another when we're tired or shaken. When we hold one another and relax into that embrace, we can feel the roots of our love.

The tree's canopy spreads out above us, sheltering us from the sun in the summer, turning brilliant colors in the autumn, tracing lacy patterns against the sky in the winter, and bursting into bloom again with the return of spring. So our marriage moves with the seasons; things change, but the essence of the marriage remains, strong and flexible, rooted deeply into the earth.
~*Ann Keeler Evans*

(Officiant blesses couple): May your marriage be "like a tree planted beside streams of water that bears its fruit in season and whose leaf never withers" *(Psalms 1:3 HCSB).*

Tree Reading 2 *(optional)*

Tree of Love
From the seed of this day let their love grow as the tree grows
Reaching down to build strong roots
Reaching out to provide comfort and sustenance
Reaching up to seek the grace of God
Let their love grow as the tree grows
Deeper, wider, stronger with each passing year~*Sandra E. McBride*

Quotes about Trees

He who plants a tree plants hope. ~*Lucy Larcom*

Keep a green tree in your heart and perhaps a singing bird will come. ~*Chinese Proverb*

The planting of a tree shows faith in the future. ~*Lucy, from Peanuts*

Even if I knew that tomorrow the world would go to pieces, I would still plant my apple tree.
~*Martin Luther*

Don't be afraid to go out on a limb. That's where the fruit is. ~*Unknown*

I'm planting a tree to teach me to gather strength from my deepest roots. ~*Andrea Koehle Jones*

Life without love is like a tree without blossoms or fruit. ~*Khalil Gibran*

If what I say resonates with you, it is merely because we are both branches on the same tree.
~*W. B. Yeats*

You will need:
- small table
- sapling in a decorative pot
- one or two small pots of soil
- rocks for bottom of pot
- two gardening trowels
- watering can(s) and water
- garden gloves
- wet wipes or cloths (to clean hands)
- aprons *(optional)*

Tying the Knot

Fisherman's Knot~True Lover's Knot

TYING THE KNOT *(Fisherman's Knot~True Lover's Knot)*

(Officiant): Today, **Groom** and **Bride** have chosen to symbolize their union by literally "Tying the Knot." And...why knot?! The knot they will tie is commonly known as a "fisherman's knot," or a "true lover's knot." It is the strongest knot known. It will not unravel, its bond will not break, and it becomes even stronger under pressure, just like their love is at its strongest when tied together. The lover's knot is made up of two individual knots, linked together, just like the "true lovers" are linked together in their hearts.

Groom and **Bride**, will you please begin to "tie the knot?"
These two cords represent your *past*—each of you as individuals with unique and special gifts you bring to your marriage. *(Couple holds up individual cords.)*

(Officiant): As you tie your pieces together, these actions represent the *present*—this moment when you join your two lives into one. *(Couple ties their individual knots, using both cords.)*

(Officiant): The completed knot represents your *future*—secure in the knowledge that your relationship will continue to be strong despite the inevitable changes life brings. Although the lover's knot is one of the simplest to tie, remember, it also is the sturdiest. As stress is applied, the knot will become even stronger.

It is the goal of marriage to achieve a blending of hearts and lives, but like the spaces between these cords formed by the knots, let there also be spaces in your new life together, so each of you may encourage and nurture the individual growth of the other.

You may pull on this cord to watch it strengthen under pressure while still allowing us to see the individual cords, just as your support of one another as individuals strengthens your union. *(Bride and Groom pull cord ends as knots slide together and "kiss," creating "true lover's knot.")*

(Bride and Groom hold up finished knot and each say the following):
(Groom): As these two strands intertwine... *(Bride):* ...so we join, your life and mine.

(Officiant): Did you notice when you pulled on your cord ends, the knots slid together and kissed, creating the lover's knot? And you see that the more tension you apply to the knot, the stronger it becomes; the tighter you pull, the tighter the knot interlocks. *(Couple pulls knot to demonstrate.)*

Groom and **Bride**, as you hold great respect and admiration for one another today, may you continue to hold each other tightly in your hearts to form a strong bond throughout your lives. Let this knot demonstrate the strength of your love, even in difficult times. And may it be a symbol of your unbreakable bond from this day forward and forevermore.

Note: Some couples choose to display the knot in a shadow box as a reminder of their marriage bond and a keepsake of the day they "tied the knot."

You will need:
• two cords/ropes of different colors (1/2" to 1" thick) to represent couple's individual lives

Unity Bouquet

UNITY BOUQUET

The "Unity Bouquet" ceremony is a good alternative to the Unity Candle for outdoor weddings where a flame might blow out in a draft or wind. There are several versions of the Unity Bouquet, but they all include the joining of family and friends, along with the Bride's and Groom's hearts.

Unity Bouquet~*Version 1*
(Mothers bring individual bouquets)

(Mothers of Bride and Groom are escorted down aisle, each holding a bouquet of flowers they place in side vases on altar before being seated. These individual bouquets represent the life of their family member about to be married.)

(During Unity Bouquet ceremony, Officiant explains symbolism.)

(Officiant): **Groom** and **Bride** have chosen to include a "Unity Bouquet" ceremony in their wedding today.

(Officiant points to mother's bouquets.)

(Officiant): The Bride's and Groom's mothers have placed their individual bouquets in their respective vases, which represent the individual lives of their children.

These separate bouquets of flowers also symbolize the Bride and Groom and the many ways in which they have blossomed and grown into the people they are today. At this time, **Groom** and **Bride,** please place your individual bouquets in the Unity Bouquet Vase.

(Bride and Groom also may have their own flower(s) and place their individual flowers into center vase, along with their mothers' flowers from side vases, creating a very special Unity Bouquet. Alternatively, mothers may come forward and place their bouquets in center vase first, followed by Bride and Groom, who place their bouquet in center of arrangement.)

(Officiant): Although each bouquet and each life are beautiful alone, they are even more beautiful when combined because, like the bouquets, the two of you are just better together than separate. May you continue to blossom and grow in your marriage as you walk down life's pathway together. And may your marriage be a sweet fragrance to all who are blessed to call you friend.

(Flower choices can have a very dramatic effect. For example, if Groom's family carries baby's breath or lavender, and Bride's family carries roses, Unity Bouquet is stunning when combined.)

You will need:
- two bouquets for mothers to carry
- two individual flowers for Bride and Groom *(optional)*
- three vases (Unity Bouquet Vase and two smaller side vases)
- table for vases and bouquets
- water *(optional)*

Unity Bouquet~*Version 2*

(Blending families~Family Unity Bouquet~Includes children)

This version of the "Unity Bouquet" ceremony symbolizes the blending of families and allows children to feel included in the wedding ceremony.

Before the wedding, the Bride, Groom and children will go to a flower shop and each one will select a flower of their choosing, whichever flower they like the best. Of course, each person will pick a very different flower. No two flowers will be alike or even a color match for that matter. On the day of the wedding, those same flowers will be brought to the ceremony by their beholders and scattered on a table around a vase.

(Before Unity Bouquet ceremony begins, Officiant will explain its meaning.)

(Officiant): Today, **Groom** and **Bride** are uniting in marriage, but they also are uniting into a new family with **Child/ren.** A family is being created today from very different people with different looks, different likes, different talents, and different interests, yet, each one very special. Each person brings to the family something extraordinary and unique, like the scattered flowers on this table. They will place their individual flowers into the vase, symbolizing their coming together as a family.

(Children join Bride and Groom around table and one by one, each picks up his or her flower and places it in vase, creating a colorful and fun Family Unity Bouquet.)

(Officiant): These individual flowers, with all their different characteristics, create this lovely Unity Bouquet, just like these individual people, with all their different characteristics, create this beautiful, unified family. Each flower and each person are beautiful on their own, but they are even more beautiful when they are combined together. It is the diversity of the flowers that creates interest and gives the bouquet contrast and color. Today, you have created a very colorful and fun flower arrangement that represents all of you, a very colorful and fun-loving family. May each of you continue to bring contrast and color into your "Family Unity Bouquet" for all the days of your lives.

You will need:
- a flower for each person participating
- some greenery or accents
- vase
- table for vase and flowers
- water *(optional)*

Unity Bouquet~*Version 3*
(Bridal bouquet created by guests)

This is a meaningful way to create the bridal bouquet. Family members and special friends are asked to sit in the aisle seats. While each one holds a flower (Bride's choice) or piece of greenery that will make up the final bouquet, they make a wish or say a blessing for the couple. As the Bride walks down the aisle, she collects all the flowers and greenery. When she reaches the front, she and her beloved tie all the flowers together with a ribbon that is tied in an eternity knot, symbolizing their eternal love.

Having your family and friends contribute to the "Bridal Unity Bouquet" is a wonderful way to include them and to add a special touch to your wedding ceremony, along with creating a beautiful keepsake for you.

(Bride walks down aisle, collecting flowers and greenery from guests on aisle seats. When she arrives at front, she and Groom assemble bouquet and wrap ribbon around stems, tying it in eternity knot.)

(After initial welcome to guests, Officiant explains Bridal Unity Bouquet.)

(Officiant): What a unique way to create a bridal bouquet! This is called the "Bridal Unity Bouquet." As you saw, **Bride** collected flowers and greenery as she walked down the aisle. These flowers were held by family members and friends of the Bride and Groom. Each person made a wish or offered a blessing for the couple before they contributed their flower or greenery to the Bridal Unity Bouquet.

You also witnessed **Groom** and **Bride** "tying the knot" by tying the bouquet of flowers together with a ribbon. The ribbon was wrapped around the flowers and tied in an eternity knot, which symbolizes their eternal love, encompassing all the good wishes and blessings of family and friends on their wedding day.

(Bride may hold flowers up to show guests the completed bouquet and blow a kiss to them for their contribution to her beautiful Bridal Unity Bouquet.)

(Officiant): What a beautiful keepsake to remind you of all the love you share with your family and friends.

You will need:
- flowers or greenery for each person on aisle seats
- long ribbon to wrap around stems and tie bouquet together

Unity Candle

Couple Unity Candle~Family Unity Candle

Reverse Unity Candle

UNITY CANDLE
(Couple Unity Candle~Family Unity Candle~Reverse Unity Candle)

Lighting the "Unity Candle" symbolizes the joining together of separate lives. It is the coming together of two families and the merging of two individuals into one married couple, a love that burns jointly.

The "Unity Candle" ceremony is an arrangement of three candles (the center candle sometimes being larger than the other two). The two side candles are lit either before the wedding ceremony begins or just before the Unity Candle ceremony. These side candles are usually, but not always, lit by the Bride's parents/mothers and the Groom's parents/mothers on their respective sides of the altar.

Lighting the Unity Candle normally takes place after the Bride and Groom exchange vows and rings. The Officiant shares a few thoughts about the unity that exists between a husband and wife when they enter into marriage, after which the couple will take their respective candles and light the center candle. The couple then extinguishes their respective candles by blowing out the flame, symbolizing they are now one. Sometimes the couple chooses *not* to blow out their candles to symbolize that, even though they are now one, they continue to retain their individuality.

Unity Candle~Version 1

(Officiant): The "Unity Candle" is a symbol of the union that exists between a man and a woman who enter the holy estate of matrimony. They are no longer two, but one. The Holy Bible says, "For this cause shall a man leave his father and mother, and shall cleave to his wife, and the two shall become one flesh" *(Mark 10:7-8 NASB)*. In a marriage relationship, a man and a woman leave one home to establish another. These two candles represent the individual homes in which **Groom** and **Bride** grew up. The center candle represents the new home they are establishing with Christ as the heart of that home. As **Groom** and **Bride** join together in lighting this Unity Candle, may we all reflect on the union created today between God, this woman and this man.

Unity Candle~Version 2

(Officiant): Lighting the "Unity Candle" is a symbol of the union created by a man and a woman who enter into marriage. They are no longer two, but one. The Bible says, "For this cause a man shall leave his father and mother, and shall cleave to his wife, and the two shall become one flesh" *(Mark 10:7-8 NASB)*. Today, we see two people uniting themselves as one —as one in the flesh and as one in the spirit. These candles symbolize that union. The two outer candles represent the individual lives of **Groom** and **Bride** and the families from which they came. The lighting of this Unity Candle not only symbolizes the coming together of these two individuals, but the joining together of their families, as well. May you all recognize your continuing significance in each other's lives by sharing with each other the light of your love.

Unity Candle ~ *Version 3*

(Officiant): When the flames of two individual candles join together, a single brighter light is created from that union. May the brightness of this light shine throughout your lives, giving you courage and reassurance in the darkness. May its warmth give you shelter from the cold, and may its energy fill your spirits with strength and joy. Now, as you light this candle, may it symbolize that today you become as one—hand in hand, heart to heart, flesh to flesh and soul to soul.

Unity Candle ~ *Version 4*

(Officiant): **Groom** and **Bride**, the two separate candles symbolize your separate lives, separate families and separate sets of friends. It is appropriate that your mothers lit these candles, as it is from these women from which the light of your life first shown forth. I ask that each of you take one of the lit candles and light the center candle together. The individual candles represent your lives before today. Lighting the center candle represents that your two lives are now joined into one light, and symbolizes the joining of your two families and two circles of friends into one.

Unity Candle ~ *Version 5*

(Officiant): The lighting of the "Unity Candle" is a reminder that the fires of love have once again been rekindled in your hearts. Sometimes our inner light goes out, but it is blown into flame again by an encounter with another human being. Each of us owes the deepest debt of gratitude to those who have rekindled this inner light. Because you have rekindled each other's flame, today you will join your inner lights into one brighter light. May the light of your lives grow and glow so others may see the flame and feel the warmth of your love.

Unity Candle ~ *Version 6*

(Officiant): This candle you are about to light is a candle of marriage. Its fire is magical because it represents the light of two people in love. This candle before you is a candle of commitment because it takes two people working together to keep it aflame. This candle is also a candle of unity because both must come together, giving a spark of themselves, to create the new light. As you light this candle today, may the brightness of the flame shine throughout your lives. May it give you courage and reassurance in the darkness, warmth and safety in the cold, and strength and joy in your bodies, minds and spirits. May your union be forever blessed.

Unity Candle ~ *Version 7*

(Officiant): The lighting of the "Unity Candle" symbolizes the joining together of your two hands, your two hearts and your two lives into one. From this moment on, the light of your love burns jointly as you walk down life's pathway together. May the path of life become brighter as the flame of your love grows stronger.

Unity Candle~*Version 8*

(Officiant): **Groom** and **Bride**, the two outside candles represent your two lives. Each light is distinct, each able to go its separate way. At this moment, you are two persons—unique, individual human beings. The same Creator who gave each of you your individuality and uniqueness is now giving you to each other. The mystery shall be fulfilled; the two shall become one flesh. From now on, what each of you has been individually, you will become together. What will touch your lives as individuals will become part of a new unity. As you each take a candle and light the center candle, let the combined fire represent the new unity being celebrated today. As the light cannot be divided, neither can your lives. May the One in whose name you are joined, who worked in your lives as individuals, continue to walk beside you in your life together.

Unity Candle~*Version 9*

(Officiant): It has been said that for each of us there is a candle, a symbol of our own inner light. But no one can kindle his or her own candle; we need someone else to kindle it for us. When two people fall in love, they kindle each other's candles, creating great light and glorious joy.

Groom, take this candle, a symbol of the inner light in **Bride**, and light it by the eternal light, with the dedication to rekindle it again and again, whenever necessary. And **Bride**, take this candle, a symbol of the inner light in **Groom**, and light it by the eternal light, with the dedication to rekindle it again and again, whenever necessary.

With these candles, we can see how to achieve a beautiful marriage. In your marriage, you will try to bring these lights, the symbols of yourselves, closer and closer to each other until they become one great torch of light *(join the flames)*—a radiant symbol of love, joy, peace and harmony *(hold flames together)*. This is the mystery of the union of two becoming one. Yet, it is vitally important to remember that marriage is made up of two people *(divide the flames, leave them lit)*, each with his or her own desires, wishes, hopes and dreams. These must be respected and responded to with genuine love and great compassion *(place candles back in individual holders)*.

We know it is the prayer of your beloved, as it is the prayer of each of us here, that you will continually light these candles of love, so there always will be light, joy, peace and harmony in your hearts and in your home.

Unity Candle~*Version 10*

(Officiant): These two outside candles represent **Groom** and **Bride**—all they were, all they are and all they will ever be. They are two distinct lights, symbolizing not only the families that brought them to this moment, but also the two unique individuals entering into the sacred bond of marriage. As they each take a candle and together light the center one, it represents the coming together of two lives in a marriage relationship. As this one light cannot be divided, neither shall their union be divided. A marriage neither results in two distinct personalities, nor the complete surrender of individuals into a partnership. Instead, it is a relationship that strengthens the individual through love, honor and respect.

Unity Candle~*Version 11*

(Officiant): **Groom** and **Bride** have chosen to light the "Unity Candle," a symbol of love and unity. Today, it also symbolizes the joining together of two hearts, two homes and two heritages into one. It is written, "For this cause shall a man leave his father and mother, and shall cleave to his wife, and the two shall become one flesh" *(Mark 10:7-8 NASB).*

Three candles stand before you. The two outer candles represent the lives of **Groom** and **Bride** and their families who nurtured them in their beliefs. Until now, both have let their light shine as individuals in their respective homes and communities. Today, as they light the center candle, they join their lights and their love in this new union as husband and wife. They do not lose their individuality; yet in marriage, they are united in so close a bond, they truly do become one in heart, mind and soul.

A famous rabbi once wrote: "From every human being there rises a light that reaches straight to heaven. And when two souls are destined to find one another, their two streams of light flow together, and a single brighter light goes forth from their united being." It is our prayer that you will continually rekindle the flame of your love throughout your lives, so there always will be light, joy, peace and harmony in your hearts and in your home.

Unity Candle~*Version 12*

(Officiant): We will celebrate this union symbolized through the lighting of the "Unity Candle." **Groom** and **Bride** come from two different families and two different heritages. We are grateful for the values which have flowed into them from those who have loved and nurtured them along life's pathway.

The heritage each brings to this marriage will continue to be an important element in their lives, but now will be shared between them. Out of these two families, a new family will be created where they will pass on the best of these traditions to their children.

At this time, I will invite the mothers to come forward to assist us in the Unity Candle ceremony. The candles the mothers light represent not only **Groom** and **Bride**, but also their families and their rich heritages. It is through their families' love and support, along with their traditions, that they have become the individuals they are today. *(Mothers light side candles, then take their seats.)*

The center candle represents **Groom** and **Bride**'s union—the union of their two lives, their two families and the rich heritage each brings to it. Please take the two candles representing your individual lives and light the center candle, which represents your marriage. *(Together Bride and Groom take their tapered candles and light center Unity Candle.)* From this day on, your two lives, two hearts and two heritages become one. May you always seek to find the common bond of love and respect. May you grow together as unique persons who will create a rich heritage all your own. And may the light of your love shine bright and steady upon the pathway of life.

You will need:
- three candles (two small and one large—Groom and Bride, plus Unity Candle)
- candle holders, tea light, lighter or matches and table

FAMILY UNITY CANDLE

You will need candles for the Groom, Bride and each child represented, in addition to the "Family Unity Candle."

Option 1 Procedure

(Groom's children jointly light Groom's candle and Bride's children jointly light Bride's candle. Then Bride and Groom take their respective candles and jointly light Unity Candle.)

Option 2 Procedure

(Bride and Groom light Unity Candle first with their individual candles, then take Unity Candle and together light each child's candle from that flame.)

Option 3 Procedure

(Bride and Groom light each child's candle with their individual candles, and together, they all light Unity Candle as a family.)

Family Unity Candle~Version 1

(Officiant): The lighting of the "Family Unity Candle" symbolizes the blending together of two homes into one home, two families into one family, _____ *(# family members)* hearts into one heart and many colors into one rainbow. Just as you light your candles together, so may your love for each other light up your lives, both individually and together as a family.

Family Unity Candle~Version 2

(Officiant): This marriage is not only the joining of **Groom** and **Bride**, it also is the union of **Child/ren**, along with those family members present, and those who are present today only in our hearts and memories. This candle before us symbolizes the merging of **Groom's** and **Bride's** pasts, and of the new family they form here today. It also serves as a reminder of their faith in God, who brought them together, who enriches their marriage and family, and who lights their pathway with love. Just as their love shines for one another, the flames that light the individual candles will burn brighter when joined together. Your lives will shine now as one family. **Groom, Bride** and **Child/ren**, join your flames and be forever united in God's love.

You will need:
- candles for Groom, Bride, and each child, plus Unity Candle
- candle holders
- lighters or matches, tea light and table

REVERSE UNITY CANDLE

(Officiant): When the flames of two individual candles join together, a single brighter light is created from that union. May the brightness of this light shine throughout your lives, giving you courage and reassurance in the darkness. May its warmth give you shelter from the cold, and may its energy fill your spirits with strength and joy. Now as you light this candle, may it symbolize that today you become as one—hand in hand, heart to heart, flesh to flesh and soul to soul.

However, the brightness of every candle illuminates even greater when it joins together with others. The family and friends who are here today are very important to **Groom** and **Bride,** so it is their wish to cause their flame of love to shine brighter by spreading it to all of you. To illustrate this love, we will perform a "Reverse Unity Candle" ceremony.

Groom and Bride, you will light your candle first, and then share your light with everyone here.

(Groom and Bride light Unity Candle, leaving their individual candles lit. They use their individual candles to start Reverse Unity Candle Lighting ceremony.)

Order of Reverse Unity Candle Lighting
- *Groom lights Best Man's candle*
- *Bride lights Maid/Matron of Honor's candle*
- *Best Man lights Groomsman's candle*
- *Maid/Matron of Honor lights Bridesmaid's candle*
- *Bridesmaids and Groomsmen each light person's candle next to them*
- *Last Groomsman lights Father of Groom's candle*
- *Last Bridesmaid lights Father of Bride's candle*
- *Fathers will light Mothers' candles*
- *Mothers will turn and light first person's candle on next row*
- *First person on each row will light candle of first person on row behind them*
- *Once first person's candle on each row is lit, they light person's candle next to them in their row*
- *Lighting next person's candle continues down each row until all candles are lit*

(Once all candles are lit, Officiant says): The flame of love and commitment between husband and wife shines bright today, but that love shines brighter because of the connection they have with each of you. Although we will extinguish the physical flames in just a moment, may we all choose to let the flame of love for **Groom** and **Bride** burn brightly in our hearts and cause us to illuminate their pathway whenever we can. May our love continue to shine for one another always.

Note: Each guest is given a small, unlit candle when they enter the ceremony site.

You will need:
- three candles (two small and one large—Groom and Bride, plus Unity Candle)
- candle holders
- lighters or matches, tea light and table
- small candles (with drip guards) for each guest

Unity Cord

God's Knot~Cord of Three Strands~Family Unity Cord

A cord of three strands is not easily broken

ECCLESIASTES 4:12

M & C

UNITY CORD~*(God's Knot~Cord of Three Strands~Family Unity Cord)*

God's Knot~Cord of Three Strands
(Covenant between God, Groom and Bride)

(Officiant): Today, **Groom** and **Bride** will "tie the knot." They have chosen to allow God to be at the center of their marriage, woven into every aspect of their lives. To symbolize that, they will braid three strands of cord together into a single cord. The braiding of these three strands symbolizes that their marriage is more than the joining of two lives together. It is a union with God, as well. So we call this cord of three strands, "God's Knot."

(Officiant): Each strand has a significant meaning:

The **GOLD** strand represents God and his love, and symbolizes that the Lord Jesus has been invited by **Groom** and **Bride** to the position of authority in their marriage relationship.

The **PURPLE** strand represents the Groom and his life. It illustrates the majesty of God as head over the husband. As **Groom** submits himself to the Lord, the Lord, in turn, will hold the marriage together through him.

The **WHITE** strand represents the Bride and her life. It illustrates the purity of the Bride of Christ. As both **Groom** and **Bride** have received Jesus Christ as their personal Savior and Lord, they are cleansed and purified through Christ Jesus.

Notice that the **GOLD** cord is in the center between the **PURPLE** and the **WHITE** cords. By keeping God at the center of your marriage, his love will continue to bind you together as one throughout your lives as husband and wife.

(God's Knot procedure—Groom holds gold ring while Bride braids three cords together. She uses a rubber band to secure cords, then ties with gold string to finish them off. They hold it up together to show guests.)

(Officiant): Today, the individual strands of **Groom's** and **Bride's** lives have been woven together by God to become one, with God as the third strand to make their marriage strong. For the Bible says, "A cord of three strands is not easily broken" *(Ecclesiastes 4:12 HCSB).*

Remember, it was God who brought you together, and it was God who taught you to love. I hope you will place "God's Knot" somewhere special in your home to always remind you of the threefold covenant you have made here today—the binding of a promise between God, a woman and a man.

Note: God's Knot may be found at **www.godsknot.com.**

You will need:
- God's Knot kit
- God's Knot explanation cards *(optional)*

Marriage Takes Three

Marriage takes three to be complete;
 it's not enough for two to meet.
They must be united in love
 by love's Creator, God above.
Then their love will be firm and strong,
 able to last when things go wrong.
Because they've felt God's love and know
 He's always there, He'll never go;
And they have both loved Him in kind
 with all the heart and soul and mind;
And in that love they've found the way
 to love each other every day.
A marriage that follows God's plan
 takes more than a woman and a man;
It needs a oneness that can be
 only from Christ—**Marriage takes three.**

~Beth Stuckwisch

Family Unity Cord

(Includes children)

This ceremony is a good way to make children feel part of the new family that is officially coming together. Three cords of different colors are needed to make the "Family Unity Cord."

(Officiant): Today, **Groom**, **Bride** and **Child/ren** are officially becoming a family. They will symbolize that with a ritual called the "Family Unity Cord."

There are three cords used, each of a different color. The first cord represents the Groom. His cord is **(color of cord)** because he brings **(color meaning)** to the family.

The second cord represents the Bride. Her cord is **(color of cord)** because she brings **(color meaning)** to the family.

The third cord represents the children. This cord is **(color of cord)** because he/she/they adds/add **(color meaning)** to the family.

Groom, **Bride** and **Child/ren**, you will braid the cords together symbolizing that each individual cord, with its own distinct color, will combine with the other cords, making a beautiful, colorful braid, just like you will become a beautiful, colorful family.

(Officiant may hold cord ends while Groom, Bride and children braid cords, or cord ends may be attached to hook or ring as braiding is done.)

(Officiant): Because three cords are used, the braided cord is very strong. The Bible says, "A cord of three strands is not easily broken" *(Ecclesiastes 4:12)*. This braid demonstrates the strength of your family and the strong ties that bind you together today.

Whenever you look at the Family Unity Cord, may it always remind you that your family is tied together in an unbreakable bond—forever!

Meaning of Cord Colors

RED	Passion, Love, Adventure, Energy, Ambition, Determination, Motivation, Power, Strength, Courage, Perseverance, Vitality, Self-Confidence, Boldness, Excitement, Vibrance, Inhibition
YELLOW	Sunshine, Optimism, Joy, Cheerfulness, Happiness, Enlightenment, Hope, Warmth, Imagination, Enthusiasm, Communication, Idealism
BLUE	Trustworthiness, Loyalty, Dignity, Integrity, Authority, Strength, Stability, Dependability, Reliability, Unity, Harmony, Understanding, Peace, Serenity, Tranquility, Spirituality, Cleanliness, Confidence

GREEN	Growth, Stability, Endurance, Harmony, Balance, Rebirth, Renewal, Health, Well-being, Good Luck, Wealth, Prosperity, Freshness, Nature Lover
ORANGE	Vibrance, Energy, Spiciness, Vitality, Enthusiasm, Excitement, Adventure, Fun, Confidence, Optimism, Inspiration, Warmth, Inhibition
PURPLE	Royalty, Nobility, Wisdom, Justice, Respect, Romance, Dignity, Honor, Spirituality, Creativity, Mystery, Magic, Independence, Ambition, Power
PINK	Beauty, Caring Nature, Compassion, Love, Consideration, Hope, Innocence, Romance, Intimacy, Tenderness, Sweetness, Kindness, Sensitivity, Nurture, Thoughtfulness, Playfulness, Friendship
TURQUOISE	Creativity, Sensitivity, Decisiveness, Strength, Independence, Cheerfulness, Inspiration, Intuition, Observance, Idealism, Protectiveness, Refreshment, Rejuvenation
BROWN	Stability, Support, Protection, Responsibility, Reliability, Security, Comfort, Practicality, Simplicity, Honesty, Genuineness, Sincerity, Endurance, Warmth
BEIGE	Grounded, Compromise, Dependability, Blend, Flexibility, Accommodation, Modesty, Conservativeness, Simplicity, Calmness
BLACK	Mystery, Boldness, Sophistication, Elegance, Formality, Class, Authority, Power, Wealth, Protection, Confidence, Concealment, Success
GRAY	Reliability, Maturity, Safety, Security, Compromise, Stability, Steadfastness, Quietness, Reservation, Practicality, Modesty, Intelligence, Dignity, Strength
SILVER	Truth, Sophistication, Dignity, Glamour, Wisdom, Intelligence, Sensitivity, Illumination, Imagination, Grace, Fantasy
GOLD	Success, Achievement, Triumph, Prosperity, Abundance, Wealth, Value, Winner, Generosity, Elegance, Sophistication, Enlightenment, Confidence, Wisdom, Radiance
WHITE	Purity, Innocence, Hope, Peace, Goodness, Virtue, Cleanliness, Humility, Tranquility, Reverence, Openness, Protection, New Beginnings

Note: Unity Cord or Unity Wedding Braid kits may be found at **www.etsy.com/shop/UnityWeddingBraids**.

You will need:
- three cords (may be different colors)
- metal or wooden ring to wrap cords around
- string, twine or ribbon to tie braided cord ends together

Unity Cross

Bride

Groom

UNITY CROSS

The "Unity Cross" is a multi-piece sculpture assembled during the ceremony symbolizing how two become one in the bonds of marriage in Christ.

(Officiant): **Groom** and **Bride** have chosen to include a beautiful, new tradition in their ceremony called the "Unity Cross." The Unity Cross symbolizes the three part covenant made today between God, a woman and a man.

One piece of the Unity Cross represents the Groom, while the other piece represents the Bride. When it is assembled and the Unity Cross is complete, it symbolizes the two of them becoming one in Christ.

(Officiant holds up outer piece of cross.)

(Officiant): **Groom**, the outer piece of the cross represents you. It is strong and bold. God created you to be the leader, defender and protector of your family. He commands you to love **Bride** as Christ loves the Church, giving yourself for her, totally and completely. Please insert your cross into the base at this time.

(Officiant gives outer piece of cross to Groom and he inserts it into base.)

(Officiant): Yet, how empty and incomplete man is without woman. God said, "I will make a helper suitable for him," and so he created woman from the rib of man.

(Officiant holds up inner piece of cross.)

(Officiant): **Bride,** the inner piece of the cross represents you. It is delicate and beautiful. God created you with such intricate detail, making you multi-faceted, which represents your many talents and capabilities. And best of all, he made you to fit perfectly inside the love and protection of **Groom**. Please insert your cross inside the Groom's cross now.

(Officiant gives inner piece of cross to Bride and she inserts it inside Groom's piece.)

(Officiant holds up three pegs.)

(Officiant): These three pegs symbolize the Father, the Son and the Holy Spirit. They represent how the Lord holds this covenant together with his love. The three pegs will be inserted into the cross, completing the sculpture and showing God's place in **Groom and Bride's** marriage.

(Officiant or Bride and Groom or parents may insert pegs.)

(Officiant): Now your union is complete in the name of the Father, the Son and the Holy Spirit.

(Officiant): Today, **Groom** and **Bride** become one. They become complete in their covenant with the Lord. "What God has joined together, let no one separate." This Unity Cross is a beautiful symbol of the "two becoming one" in marriage and of the covenant you have made with God on your wedding day.

Note: Unity Cross may be found at **www.unitycross.com.**

You will need:
- Unity Cross sculpture
- table to hold sculpture

Unity Cup

Jewish Kiddush Cup~Celtic Cup of Life

Loving Cup~German Bridal Cup

UNITY CUP
(Jewish Kiddush Cup~Celtic Cup of Life~Loving Cup~German Bridal Cup)

Unity Cup~Version 1
(Couple with family)

(There are three empty wine glasses on a table, along with a carafe of wine. Family members participate in pouring wine.)

(Officiant): As **Groom** and **Bride** share from the "Unity Cup," they share in the joy that is created when two people make a lifelong promise to each other. The two small cups represent their two individual lives. The center cup symbolizes their life together as husband and wife.

(Family member from each side fills small cups.)

(Officiant): **Groom** and **Bride**, your lives have been shaped and filled by your families, so it is a family member who has filled each of your cups.

(Officiant takes an equal portion of wine from each cup and pours it into Unity Cup.)

(Officiant): Wine from each cup is added equally to the Unity Cup, symbolizing the equal sacrifice you both happily make to create your marriage.

There are two reasons not all the wine in your cups is used. First, this is a reminder that while you are joined together, you continue to be individuals. Your individuality is what first attracted you to each other and what continues to draw you together. So celebrate your individuality and treasure each other's uniqueness. Second, your families have helped to fill your cups through the years, making you the people you are today, and they will continue to shape your lives. Just as the wine poured by your family member remains in your individual cups, so the bond you have with your families will remain also.

Groom and **Bride**, in your marriage, as in this wine ceremony, may each of your lives be perfectly combined together *(gesture to Unity Cup)*. And may your individuality remain cherished forever *(gesture to small cups)*. As you share from this Unity Cup, may it be a symbol of your commitment to each other, to your family and to your marriage.

(Officiant passes Unity Cup to Groom and then to Bride.)

(Officiant): May your union be forever blessed.

Kiddush Cup~Version 2

(Couple)

(Two separate goblets are filled with wine. Officiant pours half the wine from each goblet into a separate cup, the Unity Cup, from which Bride and Groom each sip.)

(Officiant): This glass of wine is known as the "Unity Cup," or "Kiddush Cup," and is symbolic of the "Cup of Life." **Groom** and **Bride**, as you share this cup of wine, you share all that the future may hold. The half-filled goblets are a reminder of your individuality; the single cup marks your new life together as husband and wife. As you share the wine from a single cup, so may you, under God's guidance, share contentment, peace and fulfillment from your own Cup of Life. May you find life's joys heightened, its bitterness sweetened, and each of its moments blessed by true companionship and love.

(Officiant holds up Kiddush Cup and says prayer): Blessed art Thou, O Lord our God, Creator of the fruit of the vine.

(Groom takes a sip of wine first, then offers cup to Bride.)

(Officiant): May your Cup of Life be filled to overflowing with God's blessings.

Cup of Life~Version 3

(Couple)

(Two separate glasses are filled with two different wines. Before couple is pronounced husband and wife, Officiant pours some wine from each glass into a separate cup—the Unity Cup or the Cup of Life, from which Bride and Groom each sip.)

(Officiant): This "Unity Cup" symbolizes the "Cup of Life." It contains a mixture of two wines. One is symbolic of happiness, joy, hope, peace, love and delight. The other is symbolic of disappointment, sorrow, grief, life's trials and tribulations. Together the sweet and the bitter represent love's journey and all of life's experiences that are a natural part of it. Drink from the Cup of Life with an open heart and willing spirit, acknowledging your promise to share together the fullness of life.

(Bride and Groom drink wine.)

(Officiant): **Groom** and **Bride**, as you have shared from this single cup of wine, so may you draw contentment, comfort and delight from the Cup of Life. May you find life's joys heightened, its bitterness sweetened, and all things blessed by your companionship and love.

Loving Cup~Version 4
(Couple with family)

The purpose of the "Loving Cup" ceremony is for the Bride and Groom to share their first drink together as husband and wife, and to show the coming together of their two families.

The heirloom cup is passed down from generation to generation, ensuring happiness and good fortune to all who drink from it. This is a special moment for the couple to toast their love, devotion and friendship.

(Officiant): **Groom** and **Bride**, the years of life are like a cup of wine poured out for you to drink. This specially designed cup, called the "Loving Cup," contains within it a wine with certain properties that are sweet, and symbolic of happiness, joy, hope, peace, love and delight.

This same wine also holds some bitter properties that are symbolic of disappointment, sorrow, grief, suffering, trials and tribulations.

Together the sweet and the bitter represent "love's journey" and all the experiences that are a natural part of it. For all who share the wine from this Loving Cup, so may you share all things from this day on with love and understanding.

Those who drink deeply from the Loving Cup with an open heart and willing spirit invite the fullness of life to be experienced by themselves and also by the Bride and Groom.

(Officiant pours wine into Loving Cup and holds it up.)

(Officiant to family/friends): This cup of wine is symbolic of the Cup of Life. As you all share the wine from the Loving Cup, you commit to share all that life may hold. It represents the blessing given and passed on to each participant in this ceremony.

All the sweetness the Cup of Life may hold for each of you will be the sweeter because you drink it together. Whatever drops of bitterness it may contain will be less bitter because you share them.

Drink now, and may the cup of your lives be sweet and full to running over.

(After family and friends have sipped wine from Loving Cup, it is passed back to Officiant.)

(Officiant holds up Loving Cup and says following words to Bride and Groom.)

(Officiant): This Loving Cup is symbolic of the pledges you have made to one another to share together the fullness of life. As you drink from this cup, you acknowledge to one another that your lives, separate until this moment, have now become one.

(Officiant hands Loving Cup to Bride and Groom.)

(Officiant): Drink to the love you have shared in the past.

(Bride and Groom sip from Loving Cup.)

(Officiant): Drink to your love in the present, on this your wedding day.

(Bride and Groom sip from Loving Cup.)

(Officiant): And drink to your love for the future and forevermore!

(Bride and Groom sip from Loving Cup, and hand it back to Officiant.)

(Officiant): **Groom** and **Bride**, as you have shared the wine from this Loving Cup, so may you share the fullness of life together. May you find life's joys heightened, its bitterness sweetened, and all of life enriched by God's blessings upon you always (or, and all of life enriched by the love of family and friends).

Note: For the above ceremonies, the heirloom cup or chalice may be made of silver, gold, pewter or crystal and may have two handles or none at all. The cup may be very ornate or very simple. Many couples choose to have the cup engraved as a keepsake of their wedding day and a symbol of their new life together.

German Wedding/Bridal Cup~*Version 5*
(Couple)
The Legend of the Bridal Cup

(Officiant): Once upon a time in a land called Germany, a nobleman's daughter fell in love with a young and ambitious goldsmith. Although the maiden's wealthy father did not approve of this pairing, it was clear that she only wanted the goldsmith to be her husband as she refused many titled and rich suitors who asked for her hand in marriage.

The father became so enraged he had the young goldsmith thrown into the darkest dungeon. Not even his daughter's bitter tears could change the father's mind.

To the father's dismay, imprisoning the young man did not end his daughter's love for the goldsmith. Instead, he watched as his daughter grew paler and paler as a result of the separation from her true love.

The wealthy nobleman reluctantly made the following proposal: He told his daughter, "If your goldsmith can make a chalice from which two people can drink at the same time without spilling one single drop, I will free him and you shall become his bride."

Of course, he was certain nobody could perform such a task.

Inspired by love and with skillful hands, the young goldsmith created a masterpiece. He sculpted a girl with a smile as beautiful as his own true love's smile. Her skirt was hollowed to serve as a cup. Her raised arms held a bucket that swiveled so it could be filled and then swung toward a second person who could drink from it.

The challenge was met. The goldsmith and the nobleman's daughter joined hands in marriage, and with the "Bridal Cup," they set forth a romantic and memorable tradition as charming today as it originally was hundreds of years ago.

To this day, for many couples, the chalice remains a symbol of true love, with a quote dedicated to it: "Love, faithfulness and good luck await the couple who drink from this cup."

Wedding/Bridal Cup Ceremony Procedure

- *Fill Bridal Cup by pouring beverage into hollow skirt first, then carefully fill small, swiveling bucket*
- *Couple stands close together, facing each other with just enough space for Bridal Cup between them*
- *Groom holds larger cup while Bride swivels smaller cup and they hold it up to their lips to drink*

(Officiant): **Groom** and **Bride**, you may drink to your new life together. But be careful not to spill a drop, for if you can drink from this Bridal Cup without spilling a single drop, then love, faithfulness and good luck will be yours forever! You hold the future in your hands.

(Bride and Groom drink from Bridal Cup.)

Note: The Bridal/Wedding Cup may be found on these websites:
www.german-toasting-glasses.com/german_wedding_cups.html
www.thomasdalecompany.com/wedding-cups.html
www.theweddingcup.ecrater.com

You will need:
- wine, two wine goblets and Unity Cup *(Version 1)*
- wine, two wine goblets and Unity/Kiddush Cup *(Version 2)*
- two kinds of wine, two wine goblets and Cup of Life *(Version 3)*
- wine, Loving Cup (two handled heirloom cup) *(Version 4)*
- wine, Bridal Cup (specially designed cup) *(Version 5)*

Unity Glass

UNITY GLASS

Unity Glass~*Version 1*
(Couple only)

(Officiant): Today, **Groom** and **Bride** have chosen to commemorate their marriage by celebrating their union with a "Unity Glass" ceremony.

Before them is a vessel of colorful, glass crystals. **Groom** and **Bride** have chosen colors of glass to represent each of them and their personalities in a special and unique way. Throughout their lives they have been two colorful, complete, amazing people all on their own, just like the glass. But today is special. Today they begin a new life as husband and wife, combining their personalities, and creating a new, beautiful combination of their colors into something totally unique to the two of them.

After this Unity Glass ceremony today, these colorful, combined pieces of glass will be given to a glass artisan and crafted into a one-of-a-kind glass sculpture as special as their love for one another. The pieces of their personality that complement each other will be reflected in the glass sculpture. It will be displayed in their home to remind them of their beautiful personalities coming together through their love and commitment to each other.

Marriage and this beautiful sculpture are alike. Both are examples of what can happen when raw, unfinished elements join together. They can be two separate entities, fluid and independent of each other with an exquisiteness of their own, but join them together, and the result can be stunning in its beauty, inspiring in its strength, and humbling in its function.

As with your marriage, this sculpture requires great care. Cherish it, polish it, protect it from harm. Keep from it that which can break it, or chip away at it, and it will remain a thing of beauty forever.

(Bride and Groom pour their individual vessels of glass crystals into center vessel, similar to Unity Sand ceremony.)

(Officiant): **Groom** and **Bride**, just as these crystals of glass will be fused together into a symbol of your love and commitment, may your marriage be fused together by a love that is beautiful, strong, complimentary and complete.

Unity Glass~*Version 2*
(Couple and children)

(Officiant): Today, **Groom** and **Bride** have chosen to commemorate their marriage and family through the celebration of a "Unity Glass" ceremony. This ceremony symbolizes the melding together of **Groom** and **Bride** into a new, permanent marriage relationship. Also included in this ceremony are their children. So this is not only the blending of a couple, it is the fusing together of a family as a whole. **Groom**, **Bride** and **Child/ren** have selected different colors of crushed glass crystals to symbolize their own unique, distinct personalities.

Each sparkling glass crystal represents a special moment, decision, feeling or experience that shaped **Groom**, **Bride** and **Child/ren** into the amazing individuals they are today.

Together they will combine the colored glass crystals into a common vessel. The blending of these individual crystals represents their separate, independent, unique characteristics that beautifully complement each other to create a thing of greater beauty called "family."

After this Unity Glass ceremony today, these colorful, combined pieces of glass will be given to a glass artisan and crafted into a one-of-a-kind sculpture as special as their love for one another. The pieces of their personalities that complement each other will be reflected in the Unity Glass sculpture. It will be displayed in their home to remind them of their beautiful, individual personalities coming together through their love and commitment to each other as a family.

Marriage and family and this beautiful sculpture are alike. All are examples of what can happen when raw, unfinished elements join together. They can be separate entities, fluid and independent of each other with an exquisiteness of their own, but join them together, and the result can be stunning in its beauty, inspiring in its strength, and humbling in its function.

As with your marriage and family, this sculpture requires great care. Cherish it, polish it, protect it from harm. Keep from it that which can break it, or chip away at it, and it will remain a thing of beauty forever. You may combine your glass crystals into the vessel now.

(Groom, Bride and children pour their glass crystals into common vessel together.)

Groom, **Bride** and **Child/ren**, just as these crystals of glass will be fused together into a symbol of your love and commitment, may your marriage and family be fused together by a love that is beautiful, strong, complimentary and complete.

Note: Unity Glass may be found at **www.unityinglass.com**.

You will need:
• vessels for each participant
• different colored glass crystals for each person
• bowl or vessel to hold combined crystals
• table

Unity Heart

Bride

Groom

UNITY HEART

Unity Heart~*Version 1*

The "Unity Heart" is a multi-piece sculpture assembled during the ceremony representing how two become one in marriage.

(Officiant): At this time, **Groom** and **Bride** will assemble the "Unity Heart," a beautiful, symbolic sculpture that will be displayed in their home to remind them of the covenant they are making today.

(Officiant holds Groom's outer piece of Unity Heart.)

(Officiant): In Genesis, we read that God created man in his own image. **Groom**, that means he created you to be bold and strong, to be a leader and to be a defender and protector of your wife and family. The book of Ephesians also reminds you, **Groom**, to love your wife as Christ loved the church, totally and completely, sacrificially giving yourself for her. So the outer piece of the Unity Heart not only represents your strength, your leadership and your protection, but also the sacrificial love you must show for **Bride**. Please place your heart into the base at this time.

(Officiant hands piece to Groom who places his heart into base.)

(Officiant holds Bride's inner piece of Unity Heart.)

(Officiant): Genesis also tells us that the woman was formed from man to make the man complete. **Bride**, God made you to complete **Groom**. God created you with such intricate detail to be delicate and beautiful. He also made you multi-faceted, which represents your many talents and capabilities. So the inner piece of the Unity Heart represents your beauty and your abilities that were carefully designed to complete your husband. Your heart is placed inside the protection of the Groom's heart, completing the design, and symbolizing your two hearts becoming one. Please place your heart inside the Groom's heart now.

(Officiant hands Bride her heart who places it into center of Groom's heart.)

(Officiant): To complete this sculpture, we are placing one peg in the center of the two hearts. This peg represents the Trinity—Father, Son and Holy Spirit, which shows God's place in your marriage, for he should always be at the center of your relationship.

(Officiant places peg into Unity Heart, completing sculpture.)

(Officiant): Today, **Groom** and **Bride** become one. The two become complete in their covenant with the Lord. The Bible says, "For this reason a man will leave his father and mother and be united to his wife, and the two will become one flesh. So, they are no longer two, but one. Therefore, what God has joined together, let no one separate" *(Matthew 19:5-6 NIV)*. May this Unity Heart always remind you of the covenant made this day between God, a woman and a man.

Unity Heart ~ *Version 2*

(Officiant): **Groom** and **Bride**, by sharing your vows and exchanging your rings, you have chosen to enter into the Covenant of Marriage. It is a three part covenant between you, **Groom**, and you, **Bride**, and the Lord Jesus Christ. To demonstrate your becoming one in this three part covenant, you have chosen to assemble the "Unity Heart."

(Officiant holds up outer piece of Unity Heart.)

(Officiant): **Groom**, the outer piece of the heart represents you. It is strong; it is bold. God created man to be strong and bold, to be a leader, to be a protector of his wife and family. So the outer form of the Unity Heart represents the strength, leadership and protection of the man. And yet, he is empty and incomplete without his Bride. **Groom**, in Ephesians you are reminded to love **Bride** as Christ loved the Church, totally and completely, giving yourself for her.

(Officiant hands outer piece of heart to Groom who inserts it into base.)

(Officiant holds up center piece of heart.)

(Officiant): In Genesis, scripture tells us that woman was created from the rib of man. **Bride**, the inner piece of the heart represents you. It is delicate and beautiful. It symbolizes your many talents and your multi-faceted abilities. It illustrates how God created you with such intricate detail to fit perfectly inside the heart of **Groom** in order to complete him.

(Officiant hands inner piece of heart to Bride who inserts her heart into center of Groom's heart.)

(Officiant): And now...the two hearts become one.

(Officiant holds up peg.)

(Officiant): To complete this sculpture, we are placing one peg in the center of the two hearts. This peg represents the Bride and Groom's faith in God, and symbolizes his presence in holding their love together in the three part Covenant of Marriage they have entered into today.

(Officiant places peg in sculpture.)

(Officiant): The Bible says, "For this reason a man will leave his father and mother and be united to his wife, and the two will become one flesh. So, they are no longer two, but one flesh. Therefore what God has joined together, let no one separate" *(Matthew 19:5-6 NIV).*

(Officiant): May this Unity Heart always remind you that your two hearts are now one, held together by the One who holds you in his heart.

Note: Unity Heart may be found at **www.unitycross.com**.

You will need:
• Unity Heart sculpture and table

Unity Painting

UNITY PAINTING

Unity Painting~*Version 1*
(Couple only)

(Officiant): **Groom** and **Bride** have chosen to illustrate their union with a "Unity Painting" ritual. Marriage is the beginning of a new life together. Every marriage starts out as a blank canvas, and every day is a splash of color. This canvas waits for the colors of your two lives to be painted, a new story to unfold that starts today, your wedding day, the day you begin the rest of your lives as husband and wife.

The paint colors signify the experiences that lie ahead; colors of joys and sorrows, blessings and heartaches, the known and the unknown.

These colors represent **Groom's** and **Bride's** milestones, challenges, dreams and celebrations. These are the moments…that become the days…that make up the years…that define their lives…together.

There will be places on the canvas where the colors blend and mix, flowing together, creating a new color of experiences shared.

There will be places where the colors stay separate and stand out alone and independent, yet, still a compliment to the bold color by its side.

There may be places of contrast, parts of the canvas that look dark or messy, not at all pleasing, other parts brilliant with light and definition, and some parts left completely blank and bare.

However, when you step back and look at the canvas in its entirety, you will see it is clearly an "original masterpiece" unlike anything you've ever seen before—an artistic expression with each color, contrast, shadow and blend as unique and beautiful as the couple who painted it.

So…let the painting begin!

(Couple pours paints over canvas to create abstract painting. Or, they may use a brush to paint a more realistic painting. Both are symbolic artistic expressions of their unity.)

(Officiant): May your lives always be as colorful as this masterpiece you have created today.

You will need:
- blank canvas with easel to hold canvas
- bottles, tubes or jars of water colors (may add glitter for pizazz)
- paint brushes *(optional)*
- paper towel lined tray to absorb dripping paint, with protective drop cloth under easel
- wet wipes to clean hands
- small table to hold supplies
- Bride and Groom aprons *(optional)*

Unity Painting~*Version 2*
(Couple and children)

(Officiant): **Groom** and **Bride** have chosen to illustrate their union with a "Unity Painting" ritual. Every marriage and family starts out as a blank canvas just waiting to be painted. And today, that's exactly what we're going to do.

To symbolize the blending of this family, **Groom**, **Bride** and **Child/ren** each have chosen a color of paint that represents their own unique, distinct personalities. They will take turns painting on this canvas, which represents their life together as a family. After all, we know what a colorful family this is!

What we don't know is where this paint will fall on the canvas (or off!), but it is exciting to see where it will go and what it will create. Just like we don't know what life holds for this family, it is exciting to see where they will go, what they will create, but most of all, what a great adventure it will be!

So...let the adventure begin!

(Each family member pours their paint over canvas to create abstract painting. Or, they may use a brush to paint a more realistic painting. Both methods are symbolic artistic expressions of the blending together of family. They may hang the painting in their home as a reminder of the day they officially became a family.)

(Officiant): Look what you have painted—a masterpiece! May your lives always be as colorful as this masterpiece you have created today. And may your life together always be a great adventure!

You will need:
- blank canvas with easel to hold canvas
- bottles, tubes or jars of water colors (may add glitter for pizazz)
- paint brushes *(optional)*
- paper towel lined tray to absorb dripping paint, with protective drop cloth under easel
- wet wipes to clean hands
- small table to hold supplies
- Bride, Groom and children aprons *(optional)*

Unity Puzzle

UNITY PUZZLE

The "Unity Puzzle" is a fun, visual way to symbolize your union as a couple, or as a family (if children are involved), by assembling a personalized, keepsake puzzle. There are two types of Unity Puzzles: the "Marriage Unity Puzzle" (couple only) and the "Family Unity Puzzle" (couple and children). Each one has two different versions provided.

Marriage Unity Puzzle~Version 1
(Puzzle of any shape)

(Officiant): Life is like a jigsaw puzzle. To every life there come pieces of individuals. To every marriage, a bonding of these pieces. You are a piece of the puzzle of someone else's life. You may never know where you fit, but others will fill the holes in their lives with pieces of you.

Groom and **Bride**, today, you are joining the pieces of your individual selves to fill the husband and wife shaped hole in your lives and form a partnership of marriage, which is symbolized by this "Marriage Unity Puzzle" you will put together.

God made many puzzle pieces, but only those two "cut out" for each other can fit together perfectly to create a beautiful picture. You two are cut out for each other, and your marriage puzzle has just begun. Every day, more and more pieces will be added to the puzzle with each new person who comes into your life, bringing their own dimension and color. Remember, it takes time to put a puzzle together. There are no shortcuts. It's just one piece at a time, always a work in progress, right up to the last piece.

So…let's put this puzzle together!

(Couple puts their pieces in puzzle tray.)

(Officiant): **Groom** and **Bride**, may your union here today be like this puzzle, each piece unique with its own place, yet fitting perfectly with the other pieces to form an inseparable bond and a one-of-a-kind masterpiece called "marriage."

Note: Unity Puzzles may be found at
www.puzzled1.com/unity-ceremony-wedding-puzzles.

You will need:
• Unity Puzzle
• table to hold puzzle

253

Marriage Unity Puzzle~*Version 2*

(Puzzle is a circle with God in center)

(Officiant): Life is like a jigsaw puzzle. To every life there comes piece of individuals. To every marriage, a bonding of these pieces. **Groom** and **Bride**, today, you are joining the pieces of your individual lives to form a partnership of marriage, which is symbolized by this "Marriage Unity Puzzle" you will put together.

You will notice that the puzzle is in the shape of a circle. Marriage also is like a circle. It unites those within it, surrounds each one with love, protects the hearts inside its boundaries, encompasses the hopes and dreams of the ones included in the circle, and it is endless in its continual commitment to love. So a circle is the perfect shape to illustrate your marriage and to hold the pieces of your Marriage Unity Puzzle.

God made many puzzle pieces, but only those two "cut out" for each other can fit together perfectly to create a beautiful picture. You two are cut out for each other, and your marriage puzzle has just begun. But remember, it takes time to put a puzzle together. There are no shortcuts. It's just one piece at a time, always a work in progress, right up to the last piece.

So…let's put this puzzle together!

(Couple puts their pieces in puzzle tray.)

(Officiant): There is one more place that needs to be filled in the puzzle. It is not complete yet; one piece is missing. It is the piece called "God." God must be in the center of your marriage puzzle. He is the One who holds your marriage together. If that piece is missing, then your puzzle and your marriage can fall apart. God symbolizes the final piece that makes your puzzle and your marriage complete. I will add the "God piece" now.

(Officiant places "God piece" in puzzle tray.)

(Officiant): When you put all the pieces together, they fit perfectly to create a beautiful picture, just like the two of you fit perfectly to create a beautiful marriage, with God in the center of your relationship. May your marriage be a circle of love and strength, founded on faith, joined in love, kept by God, forever together.

Note: Unity Puzzles may be found at
www.puzzled1.com/unity-ceremony-wedding-puzzles.

You will need:
• Unity Puzzle with God as center piece
• table to hold puzzle

Family Unity Puzzle~*Version 1*
(Puzzle of any shape)

(During Family Unity Puzzle Ceremony, each family member will come forward and place their special piece in puzzle tray. As they put puzzle together, it signifies them coming together to form one family.)

(Officiant): To celebrate the new family created here today, **Groom** and **Bride** have chosen a "Family Unity Puzzle" to symbolize their union and to acknowledge the joining of **Child/ren** to this family.

A family is like a puzzle; it contains pieces of different shapes and sizes, every piece being unique that fits only in its special place. Each one of you is unique also with your individual personalities, and in this family, you will have your own special place, too.

Every one of you is a very important part of this family, and you each add a special dimension to it, just like every puzzle piece is important and adds a little more dimension to the picture. But remember, a puzzle is not complete without every single piece in place. That's why it is important for all of you to be a part of this family and to put your piece in its place in the Family Puzzle.

So…let's put this puzzle together!

(One by one, Groom, Bride and children put their pieces in Family Unity Puzzle.)

(Officiant): When you put all the pieces together, they fit perfectly to create a beautiful picture, just like each of you fits perfectly to create this beautiful family. May your union today always be like this puzzle, each piece is unique with its own place, yet it combines perfectly with the other pieces to form an inseparable bond, and a one-of-a-kind masterpiece called "family."

Note: Unity Puzzles may be found at
www.puzzled1.com/unity-ceremony-wedding-puzzles.

You will need:
- Unity Puzzle with a piece for each family member
- table to hold puzzle

Family Unity Puzzle~Version 2

(Puzzle is a circle with God in center)

(During Family Unity Puzzle Ceremony, each family member will come forward and place their special piece in puzzle tray. As they put puzzle together, it signifies them coming together to form one family.)

(Officiant): To celebrate the new family created here today, **Groom** and **Bride** have chosen a "Family Unity Puzzle" to symbolize their union and acknowledge the joining of **Child/ren** to this family.

A family is like a puzzle; it contains pieces of different shapes and sizes, every piece being unique that fits only in its special place. Each one of you is unique also with your individual personalities, and in this family, you will have your own special place, too.

You will notice that the puzzle is in the shape of a circle. A family is like a circle also. It unites everyone within it, surrounds each one with love, protects those inside its boundaries, encompasses the hopes and dreams of those included in the family circle, and never, ever ends—family is forever.

Every one of you is a very important part of this family, and you each add a special dimension to it, just like every puzzle piece is important and adds a little more dimension to the picture. But remember, a puzzle is not complete without every single piece in place. That's why it is important for all of you to be a part of this family and to put your piece in its place in the Family Puzzle.

So…let's put this puzzle together!

(One by one, Groom, Bride and children put their pieces in Family Unity Puzzle.)

(Officiant): There is one more place that needs to be filled in the puzzle. It is not complete yet; one piece is missing. It is the piece called "God." God must be in the center of your family puzzle. He is the One who holds your family all together. If that piece is missing, then your puzzle and your family can fall apart. God symbolizes the final piece that makes your puzzle and your family complete. I will add the "God piece" now.

(Officiant places "God piece" in puzzle tray.)

(Officiant): When you put all the pieces together, they fit perfectly to create a beautiful picture, just like each one of you fits perfectly to create this beautiful family, with God in the center of your relationships. May your family be a circle of love and strength, founded on faith, joined in love, kept by God, forever together.

Note: Unity Puzzles may be found at **www.puzzled1.com/unity-ceremony-wedding-puzzles**.

You will need:
• Unity Puzzle with a piece for each family member, with God as center piece
• table to hold puzzle

Personalization of Unity Puzzle

To personalize the Unity Puzzle, you may add a quote, scripture verse or even include a photo, along with the names of the couple, and children, if it is a blended family. The puzzle shapes may be anything you can imagine—a heart, tree, flower, animal, house, state or puzzle-shaped piece.

Quotes about Puzzles and Family (optional)

Family is like a puzzle, it is not complete without all of its pieces.~*Unknown*

We are like pieces in a jigsaw puzzle. We all are unique, and have our own special place in the family puzzle. Without each of us, the puzzle is incomplete.~*Unknown*

It's always the small pieces that make the big picture.~*Unknown*

You are a piece of the puzzle of someone else's life. You may never know where you fit, but others will fill the holes in their lives with pieces of you.~*Bonnie Arbon*

God made many puzzle pieces, but only those two "cut out" for each other can fit together to create a perfect and beautiful picture.~*Jessica Cochran*

Call it a clan, call it a tribe, call it a network, call it a family. Whatever you call it, whoever you are, you need one.~*Jane Howard*

Family isn't just about whose blood runs through your veins. It's about who never left your side, stood up for you and believed in you.~*Adrian Body*

The family. We were a strange little band of characters trudging through life sharing diseases and toothpaste, coveting one another's desserts, hiding shampoo, borrowing money, locking each other out of our rooms, inflicting pain and kissing to heal it in the same instant, loving, laughing, defending, and trying to figure out the common thread that bound us all together.~*Erma Bombeck*

Family isn't always blood. It's the people in your life who want you in theirs, the ones who accept you for who you are, the ones who would do anything to see you smile and who love you no matter what. So be thankful for what you have. Don't wait until it's too late to tell someone how much you love them and how much you care about them, because when they're gone, no matter how loud you shout and cry, they won't hear you anymore.~*Unknown*

No family is perfect; we argue, we fight, we even stop talking to each other at times. But in the end, family is family—the love will always be there.~*Unknown*

Another thing about a jigsaw puzzle is that it takes time to put it all together. You usually know what the final product is going to look like, but you have to go through the effort of placing each piece into its rightful position. There are no short cuts. One piece at a time, it's always a work in progress right up to the very last piece.~*Ken Jacques*

Vows of Support

(Family and Friends~Community Support)

VOWS OF SUPPORT *(Family and Friends~Community Support)*

Joining of Bride's and Groom's Families
(Parents' vows first, then family/friends' vows)

(Officiant calls Bride's and Groom's parents forward or they may stand by their seat.)

(Officiant): **Groom** and **Bride,** although you have embarked on this marriage through personal choice, your marriage will be enriched by the families from which you come. I know it is important to you both to have your parents' blessing, along with their love and support.

(Officiant): With this in mind, I ask you, **Bride's Parents**, to take this man, **Groom**, into your hearts, that he might live from this day on as your son. He is dearly loved by **Groom's Parents**, and will be loved by you and your family also. Do you accept him this day into your family?

(Bride's parents): We do.

(Officiant): And I also ask you, **Groom's Parents**, to take this woman, **Bride**, into your hearts, that she might live from this day on as your daughter. She is dearly loved by **Bride's Parents**, and will be loved by you and your family also. Do you accept her this day into your family?

(Groom's parents): We do.

(Bride and Groom hug both families.)

(Bride's and Groom's parents may be seated.)

(Officiant): To the families and friends of **Groom** and **Bride**, I ask you to nurture this union with your love and understanding. Encourage them to keep their hearts open and ever tender, full of forgiveness and compassion, and full of happiness and light. Will you love them by encouraging and supporting them in their new relationship as husband and wife?

(Guests): We do.

(Officiant): **Groom** and **Bride**, may you see that, through the love you have discovered in one another, and through the love you have been given by your families and friends, you will, no doubt, find your way in this world together.

Community Vows of Support Explanation

Community vows of support can take a number of different forms during a wedding ceremony. You could ask your guests to simply say that they believe the two of you should be married and that they encourage this union and promise to support you in good times and bad.

Or, you can take the community vows a step further. Even the healthiest marriages go through the occasional difficulty, and your friends and family can either add fuel to the fire or support you through the conflict. Asking your community to support and encourage you through any marriage and life struggles can serve to strengthen your bond, as it becomes more of a bond between a group rather than just the two of you.

Everyone benefits when they are part of a community. Your family and friends are your community, and your marriage will be a part of the community as well. Odds are, most of your friends and loved ones will support you in this way even if you don't ask them to, but the ritual of acknowledging the need for that support, and receiving those assurances, can be a very important and powerful part of a wedding ceremony. Everyone who is attending on your wedding day wants to see your marriage succeed because they love you and believe in you. Having them promise to be a support along the way is very meaningful.

Community Vows of Support Options

- *(Officiant):* Do you support this union and affirm that these two people should be married today? (We do.)

- *(Officiant):* Two people in love do not live in isolation. Their love is a source of strength with which they may nourish not only each other but also the world around them. And in turn, we, their community of family and friends, have a responsibility to this couple. By our steadfast love, respect and care, we can support their marriage and the new family they are creating today. Will you who are present here today surround **Groom** and **Bride** in love, offering them the joys of your friendship, and supporting them in their marriage? (We will.)

- *(Officiant):* A marriage needs the support of a community. Will you, **Groom's** and **Bride's** families and friends, promise to support them in their marriage, loving them, and encouraging their love for each other? (We promise.)

- *(Officiant):* Now that you have heard **Groom** and **Bride** recite their vows, do you, their family and friends, promise from this day forward to encourage them and love them, to give them your guidance, and to support them in being true to the promises they have made? (We do.)

- *(Officiant):* Will you surround this couple in love, offering them the joy of your friendship? Will you support this couple in their relationship? At times of conflict, will you offer them the strength of your wisest counsel and the comfort of your thoughtful concern? And at times of joy, will you celebrate with them, nourishing their love for one another? (We will.)

- *(Officiant):* The bonds this couple has made today are sacred and holy and should not be broken. But nearly every relationship is tested at one point or another by conflict, temptation, strife and change. Will you, their family and friends, agree to help them keep those bonds holy, reminding them of their love for one another, and help them to walk through those difficult times? (We will.)

- *(Officiant):* Will you, their parents, families and friends who have gathered with them today, grant them your blessings and pledge them your love and support? (We will.) Having freely given your desire to be united in marriage, your families and friends have given their acceptance, their approval and their blessing.

- *(Officiant):* The union of **Groom** and **Bride** has joined us together because each one of us is reflected in their union. A new family has been created in our community, and we have come here today to welcome them and celebrate their new relationship. Do you, who are the family and friends of this couple, affirm your continuing support and love for **Groom** and **Bride** as they stand on the threshold of their new life together? (We do.)

- *(Officiant):* **Groom** and **Bride** have demonstrated in your presence today, the belief in their love, and the desire to live together in marriage. If you also believe in their love and you wish to add your blessing to their marriage today, please respond by saying, "We do." (We do.)

- *(Officiant):* Family and friends, you occupy an important place in this couple's lives. It is in your company that these two have learned the lessons of friendship, the tremendous act of giving one's love to another, and they ask your blessing over their marriage. Now that their life is entering a new phase, your role will be different, but not diminished. And so on this, their wedding day, **Groom** and **Bride** ask you to remain steadfast, reaching out to them in times of trouble, and helping them to celebrate their achievements and their joys. Wherever your own destiny may carry you, we ask that you continue to include them in your lives. If you are willing, please answer "We will." (We will.)

Note: Community Vows of Support may be placed toward the beginning of the ceremony after the giving away/presentation of the Bride or right after the exchange of wedding vows and rings.

Water Blending

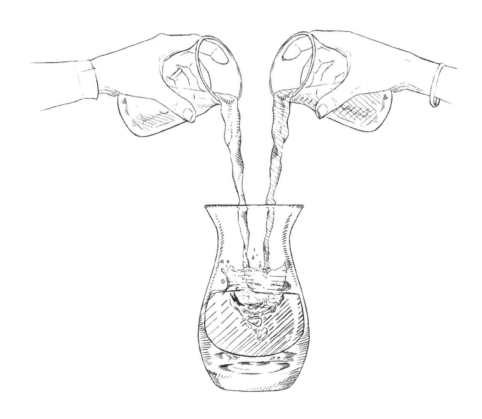

WATER BLENDING

In the "Water Blending" ceremony, different colored waters are blended together to create a new color, symbolizing the new union created this day. Choose a color for the Bride and a color for the Groom that will blend into the desired final color. *(Practice first to get the desired results.)* Note that if two colors are used, the lighter color should be poured into the container first followed by the darker color. It creates a more dramatic effect this way.

Some couples add a Wow! factor by making the water glow. Others use clear water that turns pink when combined, providing a "surprise" for the guests and symbolizing that marriage holds lots of surprises. The Water Blending ceremony is a popular ritual with couples because it shows that, together, they have "chemistry."

If children are included in the Water Blending ceremony, each child may be given a smaller glass of the same color as their parent to pour into the vessel. Unlike the Sand Blending ceremony where each child has his/her own color, the Water Blending ceremony should have no more than two colors combined, as it will otherwise appear muddy.

Once you have chosen the colors of your individual waters, and also the color of the combined water they will create, then choose some characteristics defining each of those colors that describe you, the Bride and Groom (and children), and insert them into your text for the Water Blending ceremony. (See **Meaning of Colors**, following.)

Water Blending~*Version 1*
(Couple only)

(Officiant): The Bride and Groom have chosen to include a "Water Blending" ceremony in their wedding today, which symbolizes the joining of their two lives into one.

Bride holds a vessel of **yellow** water. **Yellow** is the color of sunshine. The color **yellow** represents joy and happiness. It also stands for wisdom.

Groom holds a vessel of **blue** water. First prize gets the **blue** ribbon. **Blue** represents confidence and trust. A "true **blue**" friend is faithful and trustworthy.

Groom and **Bride**, this empty vessel represents your marriage. It is a new beginning in your relationship with each other. **Bride**, as you pour your **yellow** water into the marriage vessel, you bring sunshine, joy and wisdom to your marriage. And **Groom**, as you pour your **blue** water into the marriage vessel, you bring confidence, trust and loyalty to your marriage.

(Bride pours her water into marriage vessel first, followed by Groom.)

(Officiant): The blending of the **yellow** and **blue** water creates **green**, representing the blending of your lives together as one. The color **green** represents stability, endurance, growth and harmony.

(Officiant): May your marriage reflect all these qualities. And may your energies in this marriage blend just as equally as the water in the marriage vessel. May you always give freely of yourself while honoring the uniqueness of each other. And may this Water Blending ceremony always remind you that, together, you have great "chemistry."

Water Blending~*Version 2*
(Couple and children)

(Officiant): The Bride and Groom have chosen to include a "Water Blending" ceremony, which symbolizes the blending together of two homes into one home, two families into one family, ____ *(# family members)* hearts into one heart, and two colors into one united color —the color of "family."

Bride (and Child/ren) hold(s) the container(s) of **pink** water. **Pink** is the color of hope. The color **pink** represents compassion, caring and kindness. It has the qualities of sweetness and tenderness. And when children are added to the equation, it carries the meaning of innocence and playfulness, which should keep you "tickled **pink**" as only children can do. **Pink** also represents love and friendship, which will play the most important part of your life together as a family.

Groom (and Child/ren) hold(s) the container(s) of **blue** water. First prize gets the **blue** ribbon. **Blue** represents confidence and trust. A "true **blue**" friend is faithful, loyal and trustworthy. **Blue** stands for strength, stability and integrity. The color **blue** also symbolizes peace and understanding, harmony and unity, which your family will need in order to blend together.

Groom, Bride and Child/ren, this empty vessel represents your blended family. It symbolizes an official new beginning in your relationships with each other.

Bride (and Child/ren), as you pour your **pink** water into the family vessel, you bring hope, compassion, kindness, sweetness, tenderness, innocence, playfulness, friendship and especially love to this family.

Groom (and Child/ren), as you pour your **blue** water into the family vessel, you bring confidence, trust, loyalty, strength, stability, peace, understanding, harmony and especially unity to this family.

(Bride and children pour their water into container first, followed by Groom and children.)

(Officiant): The blending of the **pink** and **blue** water creates **purple**, symbolizing the blending of your lives into one. The color **purple** represents wisdom, respect, honor, creativity, magic and mystery.

May your marriage and family reflect all these qualities—those that you each bring to this union individually, and those that reflect the combination of your blending together. May your energies in this family blend just as equally as the water in this vessel. And may this Water Blending ceremony always remind you that together, you create a beautiful, colorful, flowing force of nature called "family."

Meaning of Colors

RED — Passion, Love, Adventure, Energy, Ambition, Determination, Motivation, Power, Strength, Courage, Perseverance, Vitality, Self-Confidence, Boldness, Excitement, Vibrance, Inhibition

YELLOW — Sunshine, Optimism, Idealism Joy, Cheerfulness, Happiness, Hope, Warmth, Enlightenment, Imagination, Enthusiasm, Communication

BLUE — Trustworthiness, Loyalty, Dignity, Integrity, Authority, Strength, Stability, Dependability, Reliability, Unity, Harmony, Understanding, Peace, Serenity, Tranquility, Spirituality, Cleanliness, Confidence

GREEN — Growth, Stability, Endurance, Harmony, Balance, Rebirth, Renewal, Health, Well-being, Good Luck, Wealth, Prosperity, Freshness, Nature Lover

ORANGE — Vibrance, Energy, Spiciness, Vitality, Enthusiasm, Excitement, Adventure, Fun, Confidence, Optimism, Inspiration, Warmth, Inhibition

PURPLE — Royalty, Wisdom, Justice, Respect, Romance, Dignity, Honor, Justice, Spirituality, Creativity, Mystery, Magic, Independence, Ambition, Power

PINK — Beauty, Caring Nature, Compassion, Love, Consideration, Hope, Innocence, Romance, Intimacy, Tenderness, Sweetness, Kindness, Sensitivity, Nurture, Thoughtfulness, Playfulness, Friendship

TURQUOISE — Creativity, Sensitivity, Decisiveness, Strength, Independence, Cheerfulness, Inspiration, Intuition, Observance, Idealism, Protectiveness, Rejuvenation

BROWN — Warmth, Stability, Support, Protection, Responsibility, Reliability, Security, Practicality, Comfort, Simplicity, Honesty, Sincerity, Endurance

BEIGE — Grounded, Compromise, Modesty, Calmness, Dependability, Flexibility, Accommodation, Conservativeness, Simplicity, Blend

BLACK — Mystery, Boldness, Sophistication, Elegance, Formality, Class, Authority, Power, Wealth, Protection, Confidence, Concealment, Success

GRAY — Reliability, Maturity, Safety, Security, Compromise, Stability, Steadfastness, Quietness, Reservation, Practicality, Modesty, Intelligence, Dignity, Strength

SILVER — Truth, Sophistication, Grace, Dignity, Glamour, Wisdom, Intelligence, Sensitivity, Illumination, Imagination, Fantasy

GOLD — Success, Achievement, Triumph, Prosperity, Abundance, Wealth, Value, Winner, Generosity, Elegance, Sophistication, Enlightenment, Confidence, Wisdom, Radiance

WHITE — Purity, Innocence, Virtue, Protection, Humility, Hope, Peace, Tranquility, Reverence, Goodness, Cleanliness, Openness, New Beginnings

Note: See links below for more color meanings.
www.bourncreative.com/meaning-of-the-color-red/
www.color-meanings.com

Inside Out

Remember the movie "Inside Out" where emotions were personified by little colorful cartoon characters? Well…Have you ever had "the **blues**," or felt "**green** with envy," or been so angry you "saw **red**?" Maybe you've been "tickled **pink**" by a "**golden** opportunity" that came "out of the **blue**." Color plays an integral role in our lives, shaping our moods, thoughts and perspectives.

Phrases with colors for use in Water Blending ceremony (optional)

RED	Red letter day/Paint the town red/Red hot/Red carpet treatment/See red
YELLOW	Mellow yellow/Curious yellow/Cowardly yellow
BLUE	True blue/Blue ribbon/Once in a blue moon/Out of the blue/Blue blood/ Feeling blue/Talk a blue streak
GREEN	Green thumb/Greenhorn/Grass is greener on the other side/Green with envy/ Green-eyed monster/Give the green light/Greenbacks
ORANGE	Orange spice/Agent orange
PURPLE	Purple prose/Purple heart/Purple passion
PINK	Tickled pink/In the pink/Get a pink slip/Rose colored glasses
TURQUOISE	Floating in a turquoise sea/Eyes of electric turquoise
BROWN	Brown as a berry/Brown bag it/Brown nose
BEIGE	Bland, boring, beige personality
BLACK	Black magic/Pitch black/In the black/Put it in black and white/Black hole
GRAY	Gray matter/Gray area
SILVER	Every cloud has a silver lining/Silver bullet/Born with silver spoon in mouth/ Handed something on a silver platter
GOLD	Golden opportunity/Golden boy/Golden oldies
WHITE	White as snow/White flag of surrender/White knight

You will need:
- water (two colors only to avoid becoming murky when combined)
- water vases/glasses for all participants (Groom, Bride, children)
- Unity Marriage/Family Vessel for blended water
- specialty waters *(optional)*

Wine Ceremony

WINE CEREMONY

Wine Ceremony~Version 1

(Common Cup of Marriage~Red and white wines combined create rose-colored wine)

(Officiant): **Groom** and **Bride**, we will celebrate the blending of your two lives into one, as it is symbolized with a "Wine Ceremony," combining two wines into one cup called the "Common Cup of Marriage."

One carafe contains red wine, representing the deep richness of the love in your hearts and the robust energy that keeps your loving relationship going. The other carafe contains white wine, fermented in oak barrels, which represents the strength of a loving marriage and a lingering taste in your soul for the love you feel for each other. You will combine the two wines into the Common Cup of Marriage, creating a rose-colored wine, which is symbolic of your blending together through a committed relationship in marriage. Some of the wine will remain in your individual carafes, symbolizing that even though you now are one, you still will remain individuals who will continue to pour into your Common Cup of Marriage.

You may pour some of the wine from your carafes into the Common Cup.

(Couple adds wine from their carafes into Common Cup.)

(Officiant): **Groom** and **Bride**, this cup is a sign of your unity. Although you are two distinct persons, both respecting the equal dignity of the other, you have chosen to unite your lives and to seek your happiness together. You drink from the same cup to be reminded you will share both pain and pleasure, struggle and hope, bitterness and sweetness all the days of your lives.

(Officiant gives Common Cup to couple and they take turns drinking from it.)

(Officiant): **Groom** and **Bride**, may the cup of your lives be sweet and full to overflowing.

Wine Ceremony~Version 2

(Common Cup~Pledge to be one blood, one family, one kin)

(Officiant): Today, the Bride and Groom will celebrate their union with a "Wine Ceremony." The Wine Ceremony embraces the traditions that began well before the medieval period. During those times a couple would celebrate their pledge to each other by drinking wine from a single cup, which symbolized one blood, one family, one kin.

Groom and **Bride**, these two carafes represent your individual spirits—all that you are and all that you have ever been. This "Common Cup" in the center is your marriage—the joining of your two lives and spirits.

(Officiant): As you pour the wine into the Common Cup, remember the pledge you made to each other today. It is the pledge of the passion of your spirits, the constant friendship of your hearts, and the deepest love your souls have to give. It is the pledge of all that is within you, the only true pledge one heart can offer to another.

Please pour some of the wine from your carafes into the Common Cup.

(Couple adds wine from their carafes into Common Cup.)

(Officiant): Now your two individual lives are combined, like the two wines in the Common Cup. Yet, some of the wine remains in each carafe, demonstrating that even as you are choosing to blend your lives together, you still are two persons who retain your individual, unique flavor.

Drink now in celebration of your pledge and the blending of your lives.

(Officiant gives Common Cup to couple and they take turns drinking from it.)

(Officiant): **Groom** and **Bride**, as you have shared wine from a single cup, so may you share contentment, peace and fulfillment from the Cup of Life.

Wine Ceremony~*Version 3*
(Cup of Life~Couple's past, present, future)

(Officiant pours wine into cup and holds it up.)

(Officiant): **Groom** and **Bride**, this cup contains within it a wine with certain properties that are sweet and symbolic of happiness, joy, hope, peace, contentment, light and love. This same wine also holds some bitter properties that are symbolic of disappointment, sorrow, grief, despair, trials and tribulations. Together the sweet and the bitter represent love's journey and all the experiences that are a natural part of it.

This cup of wine, then, is symbolic of the "Cup of Life." When you drink deeply of this cup, you invite the full spectrum of experiences into the life you will share together.

Groom and **Bride**, as you drink from this Cup of Life, you acknowledge that your lives, past, present and future, now become one.

(Officiant hands cup to Bride and Groom.)

(Officiant): Drink to the love you have shared in the past.

(Bride and Groom sip from cup.)

(Officiant): Drink to your love in the present, on this, your wedding day.

(Bride and Groom sip from cup.)

And drink to your love in the future and forevermore!

(Bride and Groom sip from cup and hand it back to Officiant.)

(Officiant): **Groom** and **Bride**, as you drink from the Cup of Life, may you find life's joys heightened, its bitterness sweetened, and all of life enriched by your faithful companionship and unconditional love.

Wine Ceremony~*Version 4*
(Good wine, good marriage~Couple only)

(Officiant uncorks bottle of wine couple has chosen and pours a single glass for them to share.)

(Officiant): A good wine, like a good marriage, is the result of many years of hard work. There is the unhurried nurturing of the vine and tender care of the grape, the thoughtful mix of ingredients, patient fermenting, yielding the unique flavors of each passing year.

So let this first glass of wine you taste together celebrate all that has brought you to this moment, expressing hope and faith in the commitment you have made here today. And let it symbolize for you how sharing the partnership of marriage not only doubles the sweetness of life, but also lightens the burden of its bitterness by half.

(Groom holds glass for Bride to sip; then Bride holds glass for Groom to sip.)

(Officiant): To the bountiful harvest of your life together. Here's to **Groom** and **Bride**!

Wine Ceremony~*Version 5*
(Good wine, good marriage~Couple with parents)

(Each set of parents brings a bottle of fine wine to ceremony and join Bride and Groom at front. Fathers uncork bottles. Mother of Bride pours a glass for Groom, for herself and her husband. Likewise, mother of Groom pours a glass for Bride, for herself and her husband.)

(Officiant): A good wine, like a good marriage, is the result of many years of hard work. There is the unhurried nurturing of the vine and tender care of the grape, the thoughtful mix of ingredients, patient fermenting, yielding the unique flavors of each passing year.

(Officiant): This wedding represents a blending of two families, the **Groom's Family Name** and the **Bride's Family Name**, separate until now, but united from this day forward. The traditions of both families have grown through time, maturing and mellowing like fine aged wine, eventually to be shared with those most precious to us. Today, the character of each family is enriched as the symbolic vines of both family vineyards extend and cross to create a wonderful new varietal wine with the union of **Groom** and **Bride**.

(Officiant to Groom's parents): **Groom's Mother** and **Groom's Father**, do you offer this couple your support? And do you toast **Bride** in welcoming her as a member of your family and promise to always love her as your daughter?

(Parents): We do.

(Groom's parents sip a toast with Bride.)

(Officiant to Bride's parents): **Bride's Mother** and **Bride's Father**, do you offer this couple your support? And do you toast **Groom** in welcoming him as a member of your family and promise to always love him as your son?

(Parents): We do.

(Bride's parents sip a toast with Groom.)

(Officiant): To the bountiful harvest of their life together. May this toast symbolize for all how the partnership of marriage not only doubles the sweetness of life, but also lightens the burden of its bitterness by half. Here's to **Groom and Bride**!

Note: The Wine Ceremony and the Unity Cup are similar in their procedures. However, the Unity Cup or Kiddush Cup is a Jewish tradition, whereas the Wine Ceremony is a secular tradition. *(See Unity Cup for more ideas for Wine Ceremony wording.)*

You will need:
- two carafes of wine (white and red), one glass (Common Cup) *(Version 1 and 2)*
- carafe of wine, cup (Cup of Life) *(Version 3)*
- bottle of wine, one wine glass *(Version 4)*
- two bottles of wine, six glasses (Groom and his parents, Bride and her parents) *(Version 5)*
- wine bottle opener
- napkin
- table to hold wine bottle(s), carafes, glasses/cups, bottle opener, napkin

Acknowledgments

To Carol Sage-Younkin, my "ghost writer" and cheerleader:
Thank you for "tying the knot" with me all those years ago—best day ever! I love you.

Beth Schmidt, our editor:
To the best "Word-Schmidt" I know. Only you can make a best-seller out of alphabet soup!

Lauren Kerrigan, our cover designer:
To our great "cover girl," you captured our vision perfectly even when we couldn't see it ourselves!

McKenna Reyna, our illustrator:
Look out world—there's a new artist in town! So young, so gifted, so amazing. Wow! Just wow!

Websites where you may purchase specialty items for your rituals:

Family Medallion Jewelry: www.familymedallion.com

God's Knot~Cord of Three Strands: www.godsknot.com

Love Locks: www.lovelocksonline.com

Name a Star Kit and Star Ornaments: www.starregistry.com

Wedding Vase: www.palmstrading.com/native-american-pottery/native-wedding-vases/
　　　　　　　　www.kachinahouse.com/native-american-pottery/wedding-vases

Hourglass Sand Vessel: www.heirloomhourglass.com

Unity Braid/Cord: www.etsy.com/shop/UnityWeddingBraids

Unity Cross: www.unitycross.com

Unity Glass Sculpture: www.unityinglass.com

Unity Heart: www.unitycross.com

Unity Puzzle: www.puzzled1.com/unity-ceremony-wedding-puzzles

Unity/Wedding/Bridal Cup: www.german-toasting-glasses.com/german_wedding_cups.html
　　　　　　　　www.thomasdalecompany.com/wedding-cups.html
　　　　　　　　www.theweddingcup.ecrater.com

Reasonable attempts were made to identify and contact authors within for the use of their writings. Thank you to the following individuals for their generosity, especially those who allowed alterations and adaptations.

Colin Cowie~(Rituals) Preface
William and Ann Corbett~(Rituals) Back Cover
Rev. Daniel L. Harris~These Hands (Blessing of the Hands, revised)
Larry James~Learn to Fly (Butterfly Release)
Jeffrey Glassberg~Butterfly quote (Butterfly Release)
Glenda Campbell~Family, A Bond You'll Always Share (Family Vows)
La Tisha Parkinson~Family (Family Vows)
Crystal Lynn Barringer~Family is Forever (Family Vows)
Carol J. Merletti~(Love Letters and Wine Box, creator)
Ned Washington~When You Wish Upon a Star (Lucky Star)
Diane Warner~(Rose Ceremony, Version 2)
Ann Keeler Evans~Tree Reading 1 (Tree Planting)
Sandra E. McBride~Tree Reading 2—Tree of Love (Tree Planting)
Lucy Larcom~Tree quote (Tree Planting)
Andrea Koehle Jones~Tree quote (Tree Planting)
W. B. Yeats~Tree quote (Tree Planting)
Khalil Gibran~Tree quote (Tree Planting)
Rev. Ann Fuller~(Tying the Knot)
Beth Stuckwisch~Marriage Takes Three (God's Knot—Unity Cord)
Bonnie Arbon~Puzzle quote (Unity Puzzle)
Jane Howard~Family quote (Unity Puzzle)
Ken Jacques~Puzzle quote (Unity Puzzle)

Scripture passages from the Bible were taken from the following versions:
New International Version
New King James Version
New American Standard Bible
Holman Christian Standard Bible
New Living Translation

About the Author

Rev. Marty Younkin, affectionately known as "Minister Marty, the Marryin' Man," has tied the knot for thousands of couples for 50 years. He has a Masters of Theology degree from Dallas Theological Seminary. He served as a Singles Pastor for many years until he worked himself out of a job by marrying off the singles and turning them into couples.

Rev. Younkin is the Founder and Executive Director of LoveNotes~DFW Clergy Services in Dallas/Fort Worth, Texas. LoveNotes is a highly respected organization of non-denominational ministers who provide ministerial services for weddings, vow renewals, memorial services, baptisms, children dedications, quinceañeras and counseling.

Marty is married to his bride and best friend, Carol Sage-Younkin, with whom he collaborated in writing this book. They have three children and live in the Dallas metroplex.

Marty's favorite quote on the definition of a perfect marriage:

"A perfect marriage is just two imperfect people who refuse to give up on each other. If you are not connecting on a daily basis with your spouse, you are exchanging a soul mate for a room mate. I will remember always that marriage, like life, is a journey, not a destination, and that its treasures are found not just at the end, but all along the way."

Marty Younkin has authored companion books to *A Wedding Ceremony to Remember*:
   Tying the Knot—Symbolic Ceremonies to Celebrate Your Union
   Knot Tyers—101 Ways to Keep the Love Knot Tied

Made in the USA
San Bernardino, CA
07 March 2019